CARS WE LOVED IN THE
1990s

T0150424

CARS WE LOVED IN THE
1990s

GILES CHAPMAN

The
History
Press

First published 2020

The History Press
97 St George's Place, Cheltenham,
Gloucestershire, GL50 3QB
www.thehistorypress.co.uk

British Library Cataloguing in Publication Data.
A catalogue record for this book is available from the British Library.

ISBN 978 0 7509 9318 0

Typesetting and origination by The History Press
Printed in Turkey by Imak

INTRODUCTION

A few years back, I was asked to provide a strict definition for a project of what constituted 'classic cars'. After a lifetime in and around older vehicles, I felt pretty confident in defining them as any built between 1945 and 1990 with a devoted following, or distinctive design characteristics. Even then, though, I had reservations about 1980s models displaying plastic instead of chrome, because they just didn't seem 'metal' and shiny enough, or were loaded down with too much futuristic trickery. Did they really count?

But time marches on relentlessly. Suddenly 1990 is more than three decades ago – a lifetime to many adults with jobs and mortgages and children. I've already written books like this one on fondly remembered cars from the 1940s, 1950s, 1960s, 1970s and 1980s. Finally, it was time to give the '90s the same treatment.

So … we revisit more than fifty individual cars that most typical drivers will instantly relate to, pick over lots of detail about what they were actually like and recall the 1990s contemporary motoring scene in five topic-based features. After all, I drove lots of these cars in the era when they were factory-fresh, and even owned a handful. We begin with a few cars launched at the tail end of the 1980s that only gained acclaim in the decade afterwards, and end with some '90s debutantes whose heydays were really the noughties.

I must thank '90s car addict Nick Abbott for his encouragement for this project, plus Simon Hucknall at Vauxhall, Oliver Rowe at Ford and Sam Burnett at the Society of Motor Manufacturers & Traders for patient answers to my arcane questions. Thanks also, to that elite 1990s band of road-testers at *Autocar* magazine, whose work has left an unparalleled resource to tap for incisive period verdicts. I trust you enjoy reacquainting yourself with these cars – some now getting pretty rare – as much as I have.

FORD FIESTA MKIII, 1989

By any yardstick, the original Ford Fiesta of 1976 must be judged an enormous success. It was the first 'super-mini' to blend the three key desirable features of the species: front-wheel drive for safe, sporty handling; a compact transverse power unit permitting maximum cabin space; and a hatchback opening right down to bumper level.

It took Ford thirteen years to take the plunge and replace its bestselling baby (the MkII of 1984 was just a MkI revamp). The company did well to preserve the predictable road manners and excellent driving position,

while using a 6in-longer wheelbase for more passenger room and extending luggage capacity by an amazing 40 per cent. There was also a choice of three or five doors for the first time.

WHAT THEY SAID AT THE TIME

'In 1.1-litre form, the Fiesta is targeted at those who rarely travel more than 10 miles per journey. It's well suited to these short trips where its light controls, snatch-free transmission and comfortable ride will be appreciated.'

Autocar & Motor magazine in April 1989 on the £7,570 Fiesta 1.1 LX five-door.

The Fiesta, in the spirit of the original Mini, was a car for everybody in Britain, and so the range quickly grew to encompass everything from grandma's 1.1-litre shopping trolley right up to the boy-racer 104bhp XR2i with fuel injection and anti-lock brakes, and the even more lairy 133bhp RS Turbo. All Fiestas were refined and very

The beat goes on: the brand-new Fiesta on police patrol.

Brits absolutely loved this new Fiesta, and the Dagenham factory was cleared of all other models so it could meet the demand; it accounted for nearly 5 per cent of the British market and enjoyed a six-month run as the overall bestseller in 1991. The 1.4- and 1.6-litre five-door models were the most popular.

This 1990 Ford Fiesta S was the mildly sporty member of a very large range.

well made, although not all were exhilarating to drive. The line-up expanded in every direction to encompass diesel engines, automatic gearboxes and a van with a commodious cubic shape, called the Courier.

In one respect, the all-new Fiesta was a victim of its own success. The feisty XR2i proved irresistible to car thieves and joyriders, sending insurance costs rocketing; so in 1994 Ford ditched the XR2i badge in favour of the more sober and toned-down Si, to try and curb the menace.

Fiesta XR2i brimmed with verve but insurers were nervous of the go-faster tag.

LAND ROVER DISCOVERY, 1989

Throughout the 1980s, Britain's infatuation with big 4x4s had swelled, even though terms like Chelsea tractor and SUV (for sport-utility vehicle) were not yet bandied about much. This was fed by a growing number of imports from Japan that started to invade suburbia, such as the Mitsubishi Shogun and Toyota Land Cruiser. And Land Rover's very belated response was the Discovery.

The first Discovery made Land Rover's dramatic, if belated, entry into the growing SUV arena.

A welded monocoque chassis-body like the 1984 Jeep Cherokee would have given the optimum on/off road compromise. Unfortunately, Land Rover didn't have the investment capital to follow suit, so the Discovery used the existing separate chassis from the luxury Range Rover

WHAT THEY SAID AT THE TIME

'It shows just how good a recreational off-roader can be. Competitively priced and more able in virtually every area, Discovery is good enough to send the Japanese back to the drawing board.'

Autocar & Motor magazine in November 1989 on the £15,750 Discovery Tdi.

with its long-travel coil-spring suspension. An entirely new body was created with several distinctive aspects, like the stepped roofline and a side-opening fifth door. Inside, two optional rearmost seats in a sideways-facing position meant the car could seat seven, and Conran Design was employed to give the interior some panache. Hence the 'Sonar blue' colour scheme and a zip-up storage bag for the glass sunroof panel.

The initial £15,750 price was identical for either a 2.5-litre direct-injection turbodiesel or a 3.5-litre V8 petrol engine. The Land Rover image and unstoppable four-wheel drive performance made it very desirable, especially after a five-door option arrived in 1990. The Discovery prompted big mainstream brands like Vauxhall to produce rivals. Its Frontera was a licence-built Isuzu rushed into production at Luton in 1991 to cash in on booming off-roader demand. Not as classy as a Land Rover, true, but, starting at £13,500, much more affordable.

If you couldn't afford the Discovery there was always Vauxhall's ballsy 1991 Frontera.

Three- and five-door options could be had with petrol or diesel engines.

WHO LOVED IT?

A Range Rover was the big off-roader people yearned to own, but the Discovery still carried British-built kudos at almost half the price. Although there was no question it could pull its weight with aplomb on a farm, the four-wheel-drive Discovery was happy motorway cruising, with plenty of room for a big family and easily able to tackle rough terrain when (rarely) called for.

MAZDA MX-5, 1989

February 1989 witnessed the rebirth of the affordable two-seater roadster when Mazda presented the MX-5 at the Chicago motor show. It was the spiritual successor to the MGB and Lotus Elan, a bold move for a company that had lately been churning out mostly dull but dependable family cars.

With a double-overhead-camshaft 1.6-litre engine at the front, a five-speed gearbox, drive to the rear wheels, a pretty two-seater body weighing just 2,070lb and pop-up headlights, the MX-5 really was a modern-day Elan. The key difference was bodywork made not from glassfibre but conventional steel.

Buyers loved to fold the hood down and squirt along country lanes with the wind in their hair. What few realised was the MX-5 owed its existence to a casual chat in 1976 between journalist Bob Hall and Mazda engineer Kenichi Yamamoto, about what sort of cars Mazda ought to be making. When the two were working together in Mazda's Californian design studio in the 1980s, they made their dreams come true, and persuaded sceptical bosses back in Japan that the MX-5 would be a winner.

The first MX-5 was on sale for nine years and brought the two-seater sports car back to life.

WHO LOVED IT?

With the MGB obsolete by 1980, and the Triumph TR7 following a year later, the 1980s had been a barren time for Britain's many sports-car fans who didn't want a Golf GTI. The little Mazda brought the roadster back to life in a confident manner and became an instant classic in the process.

The car owed more to Britain than just its early inspiration: all the prototypes, including the crash-test cars, were constructed by International Automotive Design (IAD) in Worthing, West Sussex. IAD turned the Californian design into a car ready to manufacture in Japan.

It was launched in Britain in 1990, receiving a 1.8-litre engine upgrade three years later. However, the MkI MX-5 was also astonishing for the number of limited editions offered during its seven years in showrooms – fourteen custom models that included the Le Mans, California, Merlot, Dakar, Gleneagles and Harvard.

↰ *Exhilarating fun with copious fresh air; this is the later MX-5 1.8iS model.*

➤ *British racing green with tan leather interior was among numerous MX-5 limited-edition runs.*

ROVER 200/400, 1989/90

After thirteen years in public ownership, the Rover Group – once the nucleus of British Leyland – was released from government custody in 1988 and returned to the private sector, with British Aerospace now in the driving seat.

The new owner was gladdened to find an excellent range of mainstream cars waiting in the wings, with the Rover 200 five-door hatchback launched first in 1989 and the closely related 400 four-door saloon one year later (there would also be a three-door 200). They were intended to supplant the not-much-liked Maestro and Montego range.

Rover's 200 – this is the 216GSi – arose from a happy working relationship with Honda.

The 200 design was a joint venture with Honda, whose own version was called the Concerto. Previous collaborations were sometimes troubled but this time the teams of British and Japanese engineers pulled together perfectly to create a car with Japanese standards of integrity yet road manners and, crucially, interior space to suit European expectations.

One facet of the 200 that was purely British, however, was the 1.4-litre K-series engine, a superb all-aluminium twin-cam unit. Seeing the power unit reach the streets in the 200 was a major boost for Rover. It had had to plead for finance from the Conservative government to fund its development and ensure the company didn't become simply Honda's European satellite.

WHAT THEY SAID AT THE TIME

'An excellent car, that tries hard to justify its high price. Grip is fine even in hard cornering but body roll control is a little soft. The option of full electronic anti-lock brakes is unusual in the class.'

Autocar & Motor magazine in November 1989 on the £10,418 214 GSi.

L705 AHP

➤ *Rover 400 was the four-door saloon version, here with the later 'traditional'-style grille.*

WHO LOVED IT?

After a parade of underwhelming products in the 1980s, like the Maestro and Montego, this new 200 felt like an accomplished package with its new Rover 1.4-litre and Honda 1.6-litre engines, and upmarket image. More expensive than Ford and Vauxhall rivals, annual sales averaged a healthy 110,000, helped along by diesel models using gutsy Peugeot engines.

Actually, as the 200 and 400 ranges expanded, the more British they became, with a 200 cabriolet and 400 Tourer estate that had no Honda equivalents. Perhaps the most impressive show of assertiveness was the slick, Rover-only 200 Coupé. Equipped with a turbocharged 2-litre T-series engine, it had blistering acceleration and a 140mph top speed; they called it 'Tomcat' internally, for obvious reasons ...

➤ *The 200 Cabriolet, 200 Coupé and 400 Tourer were all Rover's own adaptations.*

ŠKODA FAVORIT, 1989

When the Favorit first appeared in 1987, Czechoslovakia was still segregated from the rest of Europe behind the Soviet Union's 'Iron Curtain'. But its remoteness from the mainstream motor industry didn't deter Škoda from bucking its ideas up. The marque had been derided for years, and its rear-engined Estelle was bracketed (slightly unfairly) in the same second-rate 'pound shop' category as the decrepit Lada Riva and FSO Polonez.

In 1982, Škoda's management had finally gained Czech state backing to design a new car. With some help from Britain's Ricardo consultancy and Germany's Porsche on the engineering front and from Italy's Bertone for the styling, what they achieved was quite remarkable. The Favorit was a five-door, front-wheel-drive hatchback, with the Estelle's trusty four-cylinder 1.3-litre engine reworked and upgraded to power it, and all-round independent coil-spring suspension.

While hardly the quietest or most refined engine, the Favorit was an eager 90mph goer, with an excellent driving position, a very acceptable ride quality, and tenacious roadholding. The standard (indeed, only) transmission was a five-speed manual with a lovely light action, and early cars with an old-fashioned carburettor soon progressed to fuel-injection and then a catalytic converter.

The Favorit was Škoda's bold attempt to up its game to western standards; this is a GLX I E Flairline.

As the Favorit only reached Britain's shores in 1989, it was very much a 1990s car, and a couple of years later was joined by a five-door estate companion and then an unusual small pick-up. A Favorit offered tons more space than a Ford Fiesta for a lot less dosh, and the only area that let it down was its cheap, dated interior; Škoda obviously reached the limits of its abilities when it came to the plastic mouldings and switches ...

▲ *The Favorit estate was even roomier than the already capacious hatchback.*

◄ *All Favorits – this is the LXi E Flairline – offered five doors, competent road manners and fine value.*

VAUXHALL CALIBRA, 1989

If you thought the Calibra looked sleek then you'd have been dead right; with a co-efficient of drag (an aerodynamic rating) of a mere 0.26, it was the world's most wind-cheating production car and would remain so for a full ten years until designs from Honda and Audi finally beat it.

The Calibra went on sale in June 1989 as the spiritual successor to the Opel Manta and, like that fine machine, it was based heavily on a standard contemporary Vauxhall/Opel family saloon, in this case the Cavalier. On that basis, the Calibra initially had front-wheel drive, but in November 1990 a four-wheel drive option was introduced. It was this model that received a turbocharged version of the 2-litre four-cylinder engine in 1992, along with a six-speed manual gearbox. While the regular Calibra was a rapid machine, this new one was a barnstormer: its 204bhp of power gave a 152mph top speed.

In truth, other Calibras were more grand tourers than out-and-out speed machines, and the engine that perhaps played best to the car's strengths was the 2.5-litre V6 offered from 1993. It was powerful, refined and long-legged, and a good deal more reliable than any four-wheel drive Calibra.

Super-slippery Calibra was one of the most wind-cheating cars of the 1990s.

WHAT THEY SAID AT THE TIME

'Without a doubt the 4wd Calibra's *raison d'etre* is most obvious during a point-to-point dash across country. Outright grip is copious and cornering ability impressive. A centre viscous coupling distributes torque to whichever wheel offers the greatest grip.'

Autocar & Motor magazine in February 1991 on the £19,820 Calibra 4x4.

The ease with which the Calibra cut through the air was obvious from the fact that, even with a rather meek 115bhp 2-litre engine, it could still hit 126mph yet fuel consumption rarely dipped below 30mpg. This was also a very practical car, with decent room for four and a hatchback in its tapering tail.

➤ *Beautiful leather-covered Recaro seats and automatic transmission for the range-topping Calibra V6.*

⌄ *This is the SE6 limited edition Calibra; it remains a very handsome coupé to this day.*

WHO LOVED IT?

Among traditional coupés (and with the Ford Capri long gone) Europe had little to offer as an alternative to Japanese models like the Toyota Celica and Honda Prelude, so the German- and/or Finnish-built Calibra was a welcome arrival. Some 240,000 were sold over nearly ten years, a fair few of which were Vauxhall-branded for British buyers.

BMW 3 SERIES, 1990

A turn of decade meant a radical change of style for the smallest BMW, the E36 3 Series. Gone were the boxy contours of the outgoing car, one that had become something of a yuppie dream machine in the Thatcherite 1980s, and in came more swoopy lines with characteristically airflow-shaped sills, together with a flattened grille and twin headlights behind Perspex covers.

The basic concept, though, was untrammelled: a junior executive car with near-perfect 50:50 weight balance thanks to the front-mounted four- and straight-six-cylinder engines, and rear-wheel drive. The cars came with twin airbags, anti-lock brakes and a stability control system, this last a much-needed piece of kit if the skittish nature of the outgoing 325i

was anything to go by. Then again, as there was a brand-new multi-link rear suspension system for the range, better stability and excellent road adhesion arrived across the board.

WHAT THEY SAID AT THE TIME

'For those who want to drive rather than merely travel, there is still no saloon for the money that can touch it. The 192bhp straight-six uses variable valve-timing to provide a fine punch and a beautiful mechanical song.'

Autocar magazine in January 1994 on the £22,520 325i.

BMW launched its new bestseller with the four-door saloon, quickly followed by the two-door coupé, convertible, Touring estate and, finally, the Compact three-door hatchback. The 3-litre M-Power straight six in the high-performance M3 made it a blindingly fast car, able to rocket from standstill to 100mph in 13.1sec. Many well-off buyers opted for the 192bhp 325i as a superb small sports saloon, while the four-cylinder cars made up for their lack of urge with uncanny levels of refinement. The 325td turbodiesel won wide praise for its eager performance and smoothness.

Well before the 1990s was over, BMW replaced its 3 Series once again with another all-new model, the E46, groaning with new safety features. It was to push BMW ever further into the mainstream of the car market.

The two-door 3 Series was now known as a coupé in BMW's determined expansion plan.

WHO LOVED IT?

The steady worldwide growth in BMW sales proceeded effortlessly with this excellent car, and it became the marque's first product to be manufactured in the USA. Perhaps a little sporting edge had been shaved off (even on the M3) at the altar of greater public acceptance, but all the 3 Series cars of the 1990s were desirable.

◄ *BMW softened the contours of its top-selling 3 Series for the new decade ahead.*

⋏ *In 1997, BMW replaced the 3 Series with this new E46 model, which boasted an impressive safety package.*

FORD ESCORT/ORION MKV, 1990

Well, first the good bits. The brand-new Escort was a roomy car, well made and with pretty good roadholding. There was lots of choice, too, with three- and five-door hatchbacks, a capacious five-door estate and – wearing the Orion badge but essentially an Escort – a four-door saloon. For many British drivers with little or no interest in a car other than as a means to get from A to B in the dry, this fifth-generation Escort probably seemed all right.

⌃ *The all-new fourth-generation Escort left critics cold with its underwhelming dynamics and styling.*

◄ *Orion four-door, Escort five-door and Escort five-door estate catered for everybody.*

WHO LOVED IT?

Not the motoring media; the press gave Ford a roastin for the dismal standards of the 1990 Escort. Whether th made much difference to sales is debatable; the Esc was ousted from the peak of Britain's sales league the Fiesta, but perhaps we were all just choosing small cars anyway ...

▲ *The Escort Cosworth brought some much-needed excitement, sharing its drivetrain with its legendary Sierra forebear.*

▼ *A 1996 Escort Calypso cabriolet offering fresh air for four and a newly sorted chassis.*

Expert critics, though, begged to differ. Ford seemed to have lost its way, yielding to complacency and even cynicism. For years, each of its new cars had set benchmarks for everyday excellence, but this 'new' Escort in fact carried over harsh engines from its predecessor along with dated packaging, heavy steering and a driving experience lacking any joy. Oh dear.

Stung into action, within two years a heavily revised range ushered in responsive new Zetec twin-cam engines. The suspension was sharpened up to hot-hatch XR3i levels across the board, power steering was fitted and the anonymous styling got a chirpy makeover. They pulled it back from the brink for sure – the Cabriolet and really rather good RS2000 models helped there – although the Escort image remained forever tarnished. Another facelift was needed in 1995 simply to keep it competitive. It was, of course, a different story for the Escort RS Cosworth, which gained a fanatical following among petrolheads for the explosive performance from its turbocharged Cosworth engine and four-wheel drive; then again, it was really a Sierra Cosworth with Escort-style bodywork intended to keep Ford winning on the rally circuit.

NISSAN PRIMERA, 1990

Time to wave goodbye to the trusty but mundane Nissan Bluebird as the all-new Primera took its place as the Japanese company's alternative to the Vauxhall Cavalier and Ford Sierra. Nissan aimed to sell 40,000 examples a year, all built at its impressive British plant at Washington, Sunderland, which had opened to great fanfare just four years previously.

Nonetheless, sales were held back by a simmering feud between the Japanese company and Octav Botnar, the man who'd been selling Datsuns and Nissans in the UK since 1968. Once Nissan had taken his concession away and formed its own distribution network, the Primera began to make headway. Indeed, a Primera was the one millionth Nissan built in Britain.

WHAT THEY SAID AT THE TIME

'Extremely effective and enjoyable, Nissan is on to a winner with its British-built Primera. You are not likely to be disappointed. The ZX in particular shows just how far Nissan has come in the past two years. Its only real flaw is a paucity of rear legroom for adults.'

Autocar & Motor magazine in November 1990 on the £16,997 Primera 2.0e.

It may look anonymous but the Primera was for a time the industry benchmark in medium-sized cars. No, really.

Buyers discovered a highly competent four- and five-door family car with petrol engines from 1.6 to 2 litres and latterly a 2-litre diesel too. Well set up with sophisticated multi-link suspension front and back, the twin-cam 16-valve 2-litre engine in particular turned it into a motorway mile-eater, with sharp handling comparable to the class-leading Peugeot 405. Much was made too of the build quality, with a right-hand drive model called the UK GT exported to Japan as a ringing endorsement of Sunderland's excellent manufacturing standards.

Nonetheless, updates became a regular feature of the Primera's life, with a facelift in 1994, a totally new car in 1995 – now with multi-link suspension up-front only to cut costs – and a major refresh for that one in 1999. Nissan opened a Technical Centre at Cranfield to tailor its British-made cars for European road conditions, so it was maybe apposite that the Primera swiped the manufacturer's championship trophy for Nissan in the British Saloon Car Championship in 1999.

∧ These British-made Primeras are at Southampton docks ready for export ... to Japan.

∨ Primera 2.0 eGT in four-door saloon form in 1992 – a superb all-round performer.

WHO LOVED IT?

Nissan chose the Primera, based on its Auster model designed in Japan, as its British mainstay because it was highly competitive with the Ford Sierra and Vauxhall Cavalier that dominated the fleet market in the early 1990s. It never trounced those two corporate warhorses, but once the company car perk became instead a tax burden on employees, the Nissan reputation for all-round excellence and value had been firmly entrenched.

RENAULT CLIO MKI, 1990

By the time the attractive little Clio popped up in British Renault showrooms in March 1991, it sported a badge of honour in the form of the 1991 European Car of the Year award.

Much of the unseen hardware below the crisp new three- and five-door styling was shared with the Renault 5 that the car replaced. This meant the familiar and much-liked torsion bar/trailing arm suspension set-up, and a broad roster of engines mounted transversely across the car. This would stretch from 1.1- to 2-litre petrol engines and 1.7- to 1.9-litre diesels; and by 1992 carburettors had all been replaced by fuel injection to lower emissions. A 6cm stretch in wheelbase helped towards a much more spacious cabin.

The old 5 GT Turbo established Renault as a premier proponent of the 'hot hatchback', and the Clio carried that on. A scintillating 1.8-litre 16v/RSi was part of the original line-up. The real performance icon, though, was the Clio Williams of 1993. Named for the marque's sponsorship of the Williams Formula 1 team, its 145bhp tuned 2-litre engine gave it a 134mph top speed, frantic acceleration,

▲ *The snappy Clio was a superb all-round package and became perennially popular in Britain.*

◄ *Gold wheels and deep blue paintwork characterise the Clio Williams, one of the all-time great hot hatchbacks.*

WHO LOVED IT?

It was the first Renault to become a near-permanent fixture of the British top ten sales charts, with more than 300,000 sold here out of 4 million made. In 1994, the Clio alone accounted for 49 per cent of Renault's British trade. And no wonder: it was frugal yet fun and wheedled into the national psyche thanks to the catchy 'Nicole?'/'Papa' TV ad campaign.

amazing grip thanks to a wider front track, and distinctive gold-painted alloy wheels. Originally announced as a limited edition of 3,800 numbered examples, eventually 12,000 were built in three phases. It's still rated as one of the greatest of its genre three decades on.

The enormously popular Clio was treated to a mid-life fillip in 1994, making it good for another four years on sale before an all-new replacement took over.

A three-door 16v Clio made a fantastic everyday car for mixing city nimbleness with cross-country long-leggedness.

WHAT THEY SAID AT THE TIME

'It seems there's no magic ingredient here, just thoroughly executed tuning of dampers and springs. Quick steering (power-assisted) completes the dynamic picture and makes the RSi feel exactly as it should – like a little go-kart.'

Autocar & Motor magazine in June 1993 on the £10,800 Clio 1.8 RSi.

LIFE ON THE ROAD IN 1990s BRITAIN

In January 1991, the final part of the M40 opened, adding 45.8 miles to the motorway linking London with Birmingham. It was by far the most substantial addition to the country's motorway network of the decade which – thanks to a few small extensions here and there, plus a 13-mile upgrade of the A1 to A1(M) status in Cambridgeshire to create an isolated, arrow-straight and sometimes four-lane section – finally crested the 2,000-mile mark in 1996. That represented exactly thirty-eight years of constructing these three-lane highways, although no one held a celebration to mark this occasion; far from being loved for the freedom they provided, by the 1990s motorways were mostly reviled for hold-ups and aggressive driver behaviour.

By the 1990s, Britain's motorway network finally reached the 2,000-mile mark.

Instead, the mid 1990s was characterised by a dramatic U-turn in UK roads expansion. Ever since Margaret Thatcher's Tories came to power in 1979, the Conservative government had been markedly pro-roads. The M25 orbiting London, for instance, was the key result of the Prime Minister's cherished 'car economy'. In 1989 a massive £23bn road-building programme was announced to begin some 500 schemes, including around 150 bypasses.

⋏ *Motorways used to be exciting, now they were fraught with hazards; check out the 'classic' Suzuki Vitara in the slow lane ...*

⋎ *Thames Valley cops and their SEAT Toledo find time for a breather in 1995 during the never-ending clampdown on bad driver behaviour.*

The Queen Elizabeth II bridge at Dartford, an inelega. in the M25, here thronged with a Ford Transit convoy.

Jeeps went on official UK sale in 1992; here is a Cherokee squeezing into one of the Le Shuttle wagons for a trip through the Channel Tunnel.

The first cars to actually travel from the UK to France through the Channel Tunnel were these Rover 200s on a freight train in April 1994.

One of the most ambitious of these was the completion of the A34 trunk route, which meant putting a cutting right through the middle of the unspoilt Twyford Down near Winchester. This split opinion just as it would have done the picturesque Hampshire countryside, and a hostile 1996 campaign was mounted, famously including eco-warrior Swampy (Daniel Hooper) among the objectors. The effects were devastating as protestors clung to some of the 10,000 trees due to be felled. The road was built, eventually, but the cost of policing the protests was enormous, and the budget to construct it soared by 50 per cent. All of a sudden, building major new roads no longer seemed viable, especially as research proved that, far from alleviating congestion, they tended to lead to swollen traffic volumes. The economic recession of the early 1990s, together with growing environmental concerns, were the final nails in the tarmac coffin. Most remaining ambitious schemes were canned, and when Labour came to power in 1997 the rest were axed too.

Most drivers probably didn't notice the administrative shift of 1998, which saw 40 per cent of Britain's trunk roads transferred to the care of local authorities. But if they'd suspected that there were more lorries than ever thundering along A roads and motorways, then they were right; throughout the whole of the 1990s, British road freight increasingly switched to trucks with a much heavier payload.

Gatso speed cameras took their first incriminating snaps in Twickenham in 1992, before spreading their speed-killing ways nationwide.

One piece of infrastructure that did make a huge difference to drivers in the south-east was the brand new Queen Elizabeth II Bridge at Dartford, linking the M25 across the River Thames between Essex and Kent. The previous link was the Dartford Tunnel, which became a notorious pinch-point if anything went wrong. The bridge, hardly an elegant structure but effective enough in carrying all southbound traffic, was to be paid for from tolls, although such is the massive revenue raised that the promise to scrap the charges once the bill was paid hasn't been honoured ...

Three years later and something genuinely new came on stream – the ability to 'drive' to mainland Europe through the newly opened Channel Tunnel (the boring itself had been completed in 1990). Of course, cars and trucks had to be loaded on to Le Shuttle trains, rather than driven straight through, but it was far quicker, smoother and more efficient than ferry crossings. These did continue, but Le Shuttle spelt the end for the cross-channel hovercraft service, which was finally axed in 2000.

In March 1997, news reports relayed the scene of Britain's biggest motorway pile-up on the M42, in which eighty-three people were injured and three were killed as 160 vehicles tried in vain to avoid collisions. But throughout the decade, serious road casualties actually fell quite substantially.

In 1990, there were 336,000 deaths and injuries on British roads; 275,000 of these were mild injuries, 60,000 were serious, and 5,217 people were killed. By 2000, the overall total had fallen to 317,000, and although the slight injury total was up a tad to 279,000, serious injuries had dropped to 38,000 and deaths were substantially less at 3,409.

The figures are even more impressive when you consider there were many more vehicles around. In 1990, some 23m private cars thronged the country's roads, but by 2000 that figure had rocketed to almost 28m (the figures don't include commercial vehicles and buses). In 1992, a new twenty-group insurance system was introduced, which put up most premiums immediately, and hit owners of high-performance cars wearing badges such as GTI and Turbo particularly hard. What really made the roads safer, though, was a combination of technology and legislation.

The first Gatso speed camera (named after inventor Maurice Gatsonides) was experimentally installed in Twickenham in 1992, with their first use at a controlled junction not far away at the Hangar Lane Gyratory System (a big, square, scary roundabout). The reduction in accidents was substantial, and speed cameras spread rapidly across the country to spots where drivers had, in the past, been tempted to put their foot down.

In 1991, rear-seat passengers were obliged to wear their seatbelts (where fitted) at all times, and in the same year the MoT test took a quantum leap in stringency, boosting the roadworthiness – and so safety – of the average older car. After 1997, too, you could choose a safer new car from the off, when the European New Car Assessment Programme (Euro NCAP) was formed to conduct independent crash tests and then publish the results in the form of ratings. Australia had pioneered such a consumer-informing scheme four years earlier.

The internet-driven online shopping craze was in the future, but Britain's roads were still clogging up with courier service vans like this Ford Transit in 1996 as private companies challenged Royal Mail's domination.

As well as on-road life, Brits were getting heavily into off-road driving in the 1990s; this is the Ford Maverick, a co-production with Nissan that was launched in 1993.

On 1 April 1990, the Department for Transport founded the Driving Standards Agency (DSA) to operate alongside the new Driver and Vehicle Licensing Agency (DVLA, formerly the DVLC, the C having stood for Centre). The new organisation turned its attention on novice drivers in its attempts to cut accidents, its first move being to launch the Compulsory Basic Training system for all motorbike riders. In 1995, the DSA introduced its Pass Plus scheme so that newly qualified car drivers could hone their newfound skills, and in July 1996 the separate written Theory Test replaced random questions from *The Highway Code* that, before, drivers were asked during their full test. Then, as the 1990s drew to a close, photocard driving licences were first introduced in July 1999 in ongoing efforts to cut fraud in the twenty-first century.

With mainstream hybrid and electric cars in their infancy, traditional petrol and diesel remained the elixirs of driving life throughout the 1990s. And it was a blessed relief that cars across most popular market sectors were getting much more economical, because fuel prices jumped massively in this period. In 1990, a litre of unleaded petrol typically cost 38.37p, with diesel at 39.21p. By 2000, unleaded petrol was typically 75.38p per litre, and diesel 74.65p. Not only that but the number of fuel stations shrank alarmingly, from around 19,500 in 1990 to just under 14,000 ten

years later. And midway between these two points, on 30 September 1995, Imperial gallon measurements were seen on forecourts for the very last time.

From July 1996, all learner drivers had to pass a separate Theory Test to get on the road, where they then faced spiralling insurance costs.

ROVER METRO/100 & MINI COOPER, 1990

In the ever-precarious fortunes of the British motor industry, the Austin and MG Metro had enjoyed an uncommonly long run of success in the 1980s. By the end of the decade, though, they lagged way behind their rivals. While Rover simply could not afford to replace the car entirely, it did have its brand-new, all-alloy K-series engine range that could finally banish the ancient A-series motors the Metro had relied on for too long. These formed the basis on which the little hatchbacks would see a thorough revamp, and a change of name as they adopted the more upmarket Rover marque.

The punchy and lightweight K-series was offered in economical 1.1- and sporty 1.4- litre sizes, with a new 95bhp 16-valve 1.4 for the peppy GTi and GTa models. A new five-speed gearbox co-designed with Peugeot (which also provided the

The Rover Metro had a similar shape to its predecessor but all-new engines and suspension, as well as a five-speed gearbox.

WHAT THEY SAID AT THE TIME

'If ever a car had the Cinderella treatment, it was the Metro. In one giant leap the Metro went from very near the bottom of the class all the way to the top. High scores for handling, ride and build quality.'

Autocar & Motor magazine in July 1990 on the £9,355 Metro 1.4 SL.

This four-seater Metro cabriolet was a surprise addition to the range in 1992.

Metro's new diesel engine) helped transform the driving experience, along with a revised Hydragas suspension system, now interconnected front and back.

Despite minimal changes to styling and interior, the Metro was suddenly back in the game. There was more to come, too. In 1992 came a neat Cabriolet model, and then in 1994 a metal makeover at the front turned the car into the Rover 100. This gave yet another extension to the Metro's currency before its basically 1970s design could no longer compete; scoring an alarming one-star rating in adult occupancy crash tests undertaken by safety agency EuroNCAP saw the 100 quickly and quietly pensioned off!

It was not the only living antique from Rover to get a 1990s reboot. The even older Mini regained its Cooper performance and livery in 1990, which gave the much-loved little car an incredible ten more years on sale ...

The loveable Mini Cooper was back in 1990, mainly thanks to pressure from Japanese fans.

The Rover 100 Ascot SE of 1997 was the swansong of the venerable Metro-based range.

WHO LOVED IT?

It may have been ageing but the Rover Metro proved surprisingly popular, with some 390,000 sold, and then another 170,000 or so Rover 100s were delivered. They were still appealing cars, and the 1.1-litre models started at under seven grand, so they were affordable too. As the engines got old, though, they could be tricky, especially when the head gasket gave out ...

TOYOTA PREVIA, 1990

MPVs – multi-purpose or multi-passenger vehicles, whichever you prefer – were still a novel species of car in early 1990s Britain. The Mitsubishi Space Wagon and Renault's Espace had been on sale since 1985, and there was also the smaller Nissan Prairie. The only other option had been the Toyota Space Cruiser, but that had got attention for the wrong reason; its van-based design, with the front seats over the engine, had resulted in nose-heavy, pitching handling characteristics that some motorists found unnerving.

Now Toyota was having a second go at the market for these versatile people carriers with its all-new Previa. The Japanese company's quest for a forgiving driving experience led it into radical design territory. The 2.4-litre four-cylinder engine was positioned in the middle of the car, tilted over at a 75-degree angle so it could be tucked away under the floor. With power to the rear wheels but the radiator, air-con and power-steering pump under the bonnet, weight was evenly distributed, so the car was stable on corners.

The egg-like styling was certainly distinctive, but the Previa was all about the versatile space inside: seats for eight people, with the three-seater bench in the middle split in a two-one configuration and a facility to swing it round so it could face the back.

In 2019 Tory Prime Minister Boris Johnson was still driving a battered old Previa, a popular seven-seater people carrier.

WHO LOVED IT?

If comfort, space and versatility were priorities, or you simply had a big family, the Previa was the best large MPV. It was on sale for ten years and remained competitive with most new rivals throughout the 1990s. And in 2019, Prime Minister Boris Johnson was still using one, with rubbish-strewn interior, proving the Previa's excellent durability.

This was a heavy car, so top speed was only 109mph despite the 133bhp on tap. Options like automatic transmission and air conditioning (including an on-board cool-box) sapped the power even further, but the copious luggage room and comfortable ride were suitably good, passenger-focused paybacks.

WHAT THEY SAID AT THE TIME

'There's seating for eight, no shortage of luggage space, a soothing and compliant ride quality, and overall fit and finish that puts Renault in the shade.'

Autocar & Motor magazine in October 1990 on the £18,260 Previa.

⋏ *Super-versatile interior meant the rear cabin could be configured as a pop-up meeting room.*

◄ *Toyota's radical approach to the MPV included slotting the Previa's engine under its floor.*

CITROËN ZX, 1991

The ZX is one of those family cars that set some brilliant new standards when new, yet is largely forgotten today. For a few years in the early 1990s, the ZX outshone the Escort and Astra for road manners, equipment and gear change; it was much better value than the VW Golf, and in many ways a more sparkling all-round package.

Funnily enough, Citroën had been absent from the Escort/Golf class since the demise of its GSA in 1986; it had calculated that a BX with a small engine would do the job. The Citroën heritage was clear in the ZX's sharp and angular styling. However, it was an unadventurous car mechanically, with no hydro-pneumatic function to its suspension and a dashboard that presented a concise but conventional interface to the driver. Unlike in older Citroëns, you didn't need to learn the quirks of the car before you could enjoy driving it.

Yet enjoy it you most certainly could, with an expertly sorted chassis that made any ZX safe, refined and most of all fun to drive. There was a plethora of choices for buyers, with petrol, diesel and turbodiesel engines from 1.1 to 2 litres, while almost every model came with anti-lock brakes, power steering, airbags and electric windows. Once you'd picked your engine, it was time to choose from the four trim levels: the basic Reflex,

The ZX is now largely forgotten, but in its time it was the best car in its class for enthusiastic drivers.

WHAT THEY SAID AT THE TIME

'It's not just that the Volcane's handling and ride are unsurpassed in its class. What strikes terror into the heart of every rival is that it is still one of the cheapest cars in its class.'

Autocar & Motor magazine in July 1991 on the £12,670 ZX Volcane.

WHO LOVED IT?

Citroën splurged £700m carefully developing the ZX so it attracted buyers well outside the usual Citroën demographic, and indeed the car hugely increased the appeal of the marque. Built under licence by Dongfeng Automobile, it was also one of the first mass-produced cars to taste success in China. Some 2.6m examples were eventually made.

family-orientated Avantage, deluxe Aura or sporty Volcane. Soon after launch came a three-door option, and later still a neat ZX estate.

The ZX fostered enthusiastic, press-on driving. Maybe that's why the cars wore out and began to flunk their MoTs a little quicker than most, and consequently today are rarely encountered.

⋏ *You've pulled: the caravan-loving ZX estate was voted Tow Car of the Year in 1995.*

⋖ *The three-door Volcane was the Citroën ZX in its sportiest guise – perfect to impress a colleague.*

FIAT CINQUECENTO, 1991

Fiat was one of the very few European manufacturers to launch an up-to-date car aimed at city dwellers in this era. The Cinquecento (it's Italian for 500) took the place of the decrepit Fiat 126, which had latterly been built almost exclusively for the Polish market. And, in fact, the two-door, four-seater Cinquecento hatchback was manufactured at the former FSM plant in Tychy (yes, really), Poland.

The Poles could buy a car with the 126's 704cc two-cylinder engine suitably updated so it could drive the front wheels. For other markets, including the UK, which received its first Cinquecentos in June 1993, the power unit was Fiat's trusty 903cc four-cylinder, which itself had roots going back to the 1950s but was still lively for its size. Two years later the Cinquecento Sporting offered Fiat's 1.1-litre FIRE engine, Abarth logos, red or yellow paintwork, lowered suspension, a spritely 13.5sec 0–60mph time and endless low-speed thrills via its special close-ratio gearbox.

Of course, the reason that the Sporting could shine was the excellent engineering of the basic car. Independent suspension all-round, rack-and-pinion steering and front disc brakes were all part of the ultra-compact

▲ *Super-compact and very frugal, Fiat's Cinquecento was Europe's new city nipper.*

◄ *Garish interior options gave the tiny four-seater some individuality.*

WHAT THEY SAID AT THE TIME

'The engine is quiet, surprisingly refined, and averages 42mp making it one of the most frugal petrol cars around. On the stree the Cinquecento feels nimble and agile. This Fiat is the baby to beat.'

Autocar & Motor magazine in June 1993 on the £5,416 Cinquecento S

WHO LOVED IT?

Considering its low price and bias towards thrift, it seems odd Fiat didn't sell more than 1.2m of these over seven years. Then again, it was strictly an urban runabout, or else a meagre-power first car for teenagers. That's how one was portrayed to hilarious effect in the cult sitcom *The Inbetweeners* in 2011, where its lowly status was roundly mocked ...

drivetrain. Nor had safety been overlooked, with side-impact beams in the doors. Meanwhile, anxious to allay memories of rusty small Fiats of yore, all the body panels were of galvanised steel. Among the desirable options on offer were a full-length fabric sunroof and air conditioning.

Interestingly, Fiat also offered an electric Cinquecento, with either lead-acid or nickel-cadmium batteries. The Elettra model was surprisingly popular, with its range of 125 miles, and many were bought by local authorities and other governmental agencies in Italy. However, as all of the cargo space was needed to house the batteries, it was strictly a two-seater car.

◄ *Boxy back end didn't conceal much cargo space as all the interior was taken up by seats.*

▼ *Peppy performance from the Cinquecento Sporting, with historic Abarth livery.*

PEUGEOT 106, 1991 & CITROËN SAXO, 1996

There is a hushed reverence among hot-hatch con-noisseurs for the Peugeot 106 Rallye even today. Intro-duced in 1994, this sparsely equipped three-door had a fuel-injected 1.3-litre TU-series engine boasting an artfully tuned eight-valve engine with high-compres-sion cylinder head. It could be revved to 7,200rpm, and the 100bhp on tap, through a nimble chassis with taut suspension (front strut/rear trailing arm and torsion bar) made the lightweight car – with its red seatbelts and white-painted steel wheels – scintillatingly good fun.

Limited numbers of this model were built to quality the 106 as a grassroots rally car. Still, it drew its qual-ities from the basic 106, which was intended as Peu-geot's economy offering. The 106 was derived from the humble Citroen AX but was safer and more solid; it gradually replaced the legendary 205 and was locked in mortal combat with Renault's recent Clio.

Most of them had low-power 1.1-litre carburettor petrol engines and were pretty basic, with painted metal a feature of the cabin. Probably for that reason there was almost always a distracting limited edition variant available. Because of right-hand drive con-version complications, British cars could never come with power steering or air conditioning. There was

Peugeot 106 Rallye, with its white-painted steel wheels, is remembered for its astonishing performance.

Citroën's Saxo – this is the ultra-sporty VTS – was closely based on the 106 and enjoyed a long life on sale.

WHAT THEY SAID AT THE TIME

'The sheer intensity and balance of its virtues: it can tackle a twisty road as a whole rather than a bend at a time; the way it provides a supple ride with iron control; the way it packs so much space into such a compact shape.'

Autocar & Motor magazine in December 1991 on the £10,395 106 XSi.

also a 1.4 diesel and fuel-injected petrol, while a 1.6-litre fuel-injected motor turned the 1995 XSi into a 120mph car.

In 1996, Peugeot used the 106 as the basis for the new Citroën Saxo, at the same time sprucing up its 106 with sharper looks, more kit, power steering at last, and fuel-injected engines across the board. There was now a GTi model with a 16-valve 1.6 engine ... but it was the 1.6-litre Phase 2 Rallye that still held the candle for pure performance car geeks.

WHO LOVED IT?

The 106 became the eleventh bestselling car in Britain in 1993, and its popularity meant it avoided the axe when the 206 arrived in 1998. Indeed, as production didn't finish until 2003, the 106 became one of the longest-lived of late twentieth-century popular cars. From January 2001 it even came with a three-year warranty.

Most 106s were frugal town cars although they were all fun to own.

VAUXHALL ASTRA MKIII, 1991 & MKIV, 1998

With the once-dominant Escort reeling from a critical rubbishing, the third-generation Astra could get off to a flying start in 1991. Visually, it was an accomplished evolution of the very successful MkII, with its more aerodynamic lines and taller, wider and longer stance enclosing a more roomy and comfortable cabin.

Unseen by the car buyer was a vastly superior safety package, with side-impact bars, a safety cage that was 34 per cent stronger, and mechanical seatbelt pre-tensioners front and back. In officially observed crash tests, the Astra performed better than most rivals and, from 1994, included standard or optional airbags on almost all versions.

The Astra was not above criticism. The 1.7-litre diesel engine created a performance laggard, even if 47mpg was easily possible, while the lifeless steering and jumpy ride in the 150bhp 2-litre GSi 16v performance model stopped it posing a serious threat to the Golf MkIII GTI. Nonetheless, by far the most numerous were the 1.4- and 1.6-litre models, and they were solid performers as three- or five-door hatchbacks, four-door saloons and five-door estates. A big revamp in 1994 upgraded the entire sprawling range with new Ecotec engines and kept the Astra a class frontrunner until 1998.

WHO LOVED IT?

By and large, the Astra typified competence and value in the family hatchback sector. It was rewarded by massive UK sales of more than 600,000 and a permanent place in the top ten national bestsellers league. The British Astra name was also adopted for the identical Opel range sold in mainland Europe, replacing the Kadett sub-brand after fifty-five years.

Okay, so hardly the most exciting car, but this new well-made Astra had no serious drawbacks.

In that year the MkIV Astra started to flow down the production line at Vauxhall's Ellesmere Port factory on Merseyside. Apart from the snazzy, Bertone-built Coupé and Cabriolet, it was a sober-looking car, but it was jam-packed with extremely worthwhile attributes.

A fully galvanised body structure assured a long life, build quality and comfort were excellent, and in 2002 the 1.7 CDTi became the first comparable car to meet all the rigorous new Euro 4 emissions regulations. Consequently, the MkIV was a top pick among fleet buyers.

WHAT THEY SAID AT THE TIME

'Where the Astra is good, it's very good: roomy, practical, refined at speed, well put together and outstandingly economical. Groomed as a best-seller, [it] goes about its business with a wide-ranging brief.'

Autocar & Motor magazine in October 1991 on the £11,030 Astra 1.4 GLS.

↗ *The attractive four-seater Astra cabriolet, this one a 2.0i, was built in Italy by Bertone.*

◄ *The Astra MkIV arrived in 1998, these ones departing the Ellesmere Port factory by rail.*

VOLKSWAGEN GOLF MKIII, 1991 & MKIV, 1997

If you've enjoyed reacquainting yourself with the Citroën ZX and Vauxhall Astra on previous pages, now meet the car they tried to beat: the Volkswagen Golf MkIII. The outgoing Golf had met with astounding popularity, with more than 6.3m examples delivered worldwide. Now the success story looked set for a replay as the new car – slightly bigger and chubbier looking – elbowed ZX and Astra aside to become the 1992 European Car of the Year. It was the first VW ever to claim the gong, awarded by a Europe-wide panel of seasoned expert judges.

WHAT THEY SAID AT THE TIME

'The TDI isn't quite so quick against the clock, but for real-world in-gear performance it's virtually as quick as an eight-valve GTI, an extraordinary achievement. Throttle response below 2000rpm is also the best of any small turbodiesel we've tried.'

Autocar magazine in May 1994 on the £13,446 Golf TDI GL.

Volkswagen's third-generation Golf was one of Europe's best-loved family hatchbacks.

The cabriolet with a fixed roll-over bar was a VW tradition, redesigned for the Golf MkIII.

The nucleus of wild-eyed Golf fanatics found this new MkIII model underwhelming, and there was no doubt rivals such as the ZX were more exhilarating to drive. But then there was the by-now legendary Golf quality and solidity. These facets proved irresistible to potential buyers – as did the higher second-hand value the cars retained – and at 4.8m sales were enormous everywhere.

Cabriolet. There was a conventional four-door saloon, the Vento, and the first ever Golf estate. Even the lowly models were relatively expensive, but for the money you received a car of superior quality that was secure and enjoyable to drive.

VW replaced the entire car again before the 1990s were out. The broader, more capacious MkIV took the Golf progressively upmarket, stepping away from the ethos that a Golf was an everyman product. Nonetheless, it became the top-selling car across the whole of Europe in 2001.

Adopting the zeitgeist of the time, there was a new focus on safety. Airbags were standard from the off, and anti-lock brakes routinely fitted from 1996. In 1993, VW launched a direct-injection diesel engine in the Golf. Indeed, every UK model had fuel-injection and a catalytic converter to cut emissions; the diesel-engined Ecomatic had a novel mechanism to kill the engine at standstill, and VW made a few electric Golfs too, called CitySTROmers.

You paid a big premium to own a GTI with an 8- or 16-valve 2-litre engine, the luxurious VR6, or the

In 1997 VW overhauled the Golf once again for the bigger, broader MkIV, here seen in range-topping R32 form.

FORD MONDEO, 1992

'Mondeo Man' became a seminal figure in the Britain of the late 1990s. He was encapsulated by Tony Blair, then the Labour Leader of the Opposition, in a 1996 conference speech. The fellow was the imaginary swing voter whose dad voted Labour but he himself had become a Tory as he bought his council house, owned his own car in the Sierra/Mondeo bracket, and worked on a self-employed basis in construction. Drawn from a much wider background than the 'Essex Man' of old, Labour needed this get-on-in-life character to switch his voting patterns to gain power. And the party's policies persuaded him to do just that for Labour's election victory a year later.

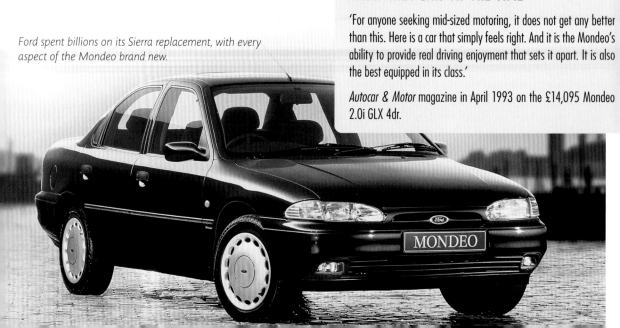

Ford spent billions on its Sierra replacement, with every aspect of the Mondeo brand new.

WHAT THEY SAID AT THE TIME

'For anyone seeking mid-sized motoring, it does not get any better than this. Here is a car that simply feels right. And it is the Mondeo's ability to provide real driving enjoyment that sets it apart. It is also the best equipped in its class.'

Autocar & Motor magazine in April 1993 on the £14,095 Mondeo 2.0i GLX 4dr.

WHO LOVED IT?

Excellent car though it was, the Mondeo had a fight on its hands. Company car orders were thinning as perks were starting to be taxed; buyers were going for smaller cars and choosing more upmarket nameplates than boring old Ford. Almost 334,000 were sold in 1993–95 before a big revamp to sustain buyer interest, after which some 389,000 more were sold up to 1999.

So much for the notional owner; what of the machine itself? It was a crucial car for Ford, and the company is thought to have spent £4bn on the project – it remains one of the most expensive of all time. Codenamed CDW27, the plan was to create a single model for global sale, although eventually US versions were substantially different to suit local tastes. The project was headquartered at Ford's Essex research centre, and the Nissan Primera was apparently used as a benchmark.

In contrast to the Sierra it replaced, the Mondeo was front-wheel drive. It came as a four-door saloon, five-door hatchback and five-door estate, with 1.6-, 1.8- and 2-litre four-cylinder or 2.5-litre V6 engines at first. There were all-new transmissions and suspension systems with front and rear subframes that provided excellent handling and comfort standards. Every Mondeo sold in Europe was built in Belgium, and the range was noteworthy for being first to offer a driver's airbag in even the humblest models.

↖ *Long haul: the Ghia X estate was the plush Mondeo for those with a lot on their plate.*

↓ *This facelift arrived in 1996 to keep Tony Blair's cherished swing voters on side ...*

NISSAN MICRA, 1992

Britain's leading granny mobile is still, today, a familiar sight around the country's retirement hotspots and quieter suburbs, almost three decades after it made its debut. In fact, all those elderly motorists know a good thing when they see one. This K11-model Micra was one of the best built, most refined and least troublesome small cars you could buy. What it lacked in sex appeal it more than made up for with paltry running costs.

The brand-new range of British-built Micras, all with 16-valve twin-cam engines.

Grey's anatomy; Britain's oldies knew a good thing when they saw one and flocked to the reliable new Micra.

WHO LOVED IT?

Britain's armies of oldies loved the Micra for its compact size and utterly dependable nature. At the other end of the scale, it quickly became a commonplace driving-school car and, as a consequence, a first choice for many newly qualified drivers in towns and cities all over the land. No wonder the car was on sale for ten straight years with just a few visual tweaks and tiny engine modifications to keep it fresh.

▲ Easy to park and even easier to live with, the Micra was perfect for tight budgets.

The smooth but upright styling drew inspiration from some of Nissan's limited production 'retro' cars of the late 1980s, in particular the Be-1, with a deliberate emphasis on smooth curves inside and out. Under the stubby bonnet, though, it was bang up-to-date, with brand-new 16-valve all-aluminium engines in 1.0- and 1.3-litre sizes, all sporting fuel injection and catalytic converters for clean and thrifty motoring. As well as the standard five-speed gearbox came a continuously variable automatic transmission, and features including a driver's airbag, power steering, central locking and air-con were all offered in the higher echelons of the range, which also included a 1.5-litre diesel for European markets with a Peugeot motor.

The little Nissan was a real shot in the arm for Britain's motor industry, joining the Primera in a much-enlarged Sunderland factory where the bodies and the engines were manufactured. The wraps came off the car in January 1992, and it was in Britain's Nissan showrooms nine months later. By the end of that year, its British origins meant it was also brandishing the European Car of the Year award, becoming the first Japanese-designed model (it was known as the Nissan March in Japan) ever to merit the prize.

▼ The retro-styled Nissan Be-1 of 1987 had a strong influence on the new, rounded Micra's shape.

TOYOTA CARINA E, 1992 & AVENSIS, 1998

This outwardly unremarkable family car from Toyota is actually a vehicle of historical importance. The Carina E was the first car from the marque to be built at the company's new British plant at Burnaston, Derbyshire, with engines from its other new factory in Deeside, North Wales. Toyota, in fact, has sunk £2.75bn into British car-making, and it all began with this Carina E, the very first of which was completed on 16 December 1992.

The 'E' part stood for Europe, because this version of the Carina (although, confusingly, the car was called the Corona in Japan, where it was designed) was finessed for markets across the territory. It was an entirely competent front-wheel drive alternative to the Ford Mondeo and Vauxhall Cavalier, then very much the mainstream in British motoring. Like those two, it came as a four-door saloon, five-door hatchback or five-door estate. You

▲ Here is the full title of this worthy machine: Toyota Carina E 2.0 diesel turbo five-door.

▼ A four-door Carina with a 1.8 petrol engine – significant as the first British-made Toyota.

WHAT THEY SAID AT THE TIME

'The problem is that the saloon on which it's based is undistinguished. The plus points are its performance – it out-sprints its Ford and Nissan rivals, for example – and, despite this, its first-rate fuel economy.'

Autocar & Motor magazine in July 1993 on the £14,814 Carina E 2.0 GLi estate.

could have the Xi trim as a 1.6-litre, XLi as a 1.6 or 1.8, the SLi as a 1.8, and the GLi with any of the engine sizes. Topping the array was the 2-litre GTi or Executive (but not as estates), while there were also 2-litre diesels in XLD and GLD specification. Phew.

The Carina was well attuned to British motoring life, and a sensible way for Toyota to establish itself as a European carmaker before adding the Corolla to Burnaston's output. The Carina E itself lasted until 1997, when it was supplanted by the Avensis. You may have barely noticed it, so cautious was the evolution, but every body panel was new despite the engine range carrying on virtually unaltered.

WHO LOVED IT?

The UK line-up, with its myriad specification choices, reflected the intricacies of the achievement levels of the company-car pecking order. All trim levels were renamed in 1996, too, just to make the head spin even further when consulting the Toyota salesman. Carina drivers made their detail choices carefully because comfort, equipment, refinement and quality were their guides, and not driving verve.

A Carina revamp in 1998 turned it into the Avensis, shown here in estate form.

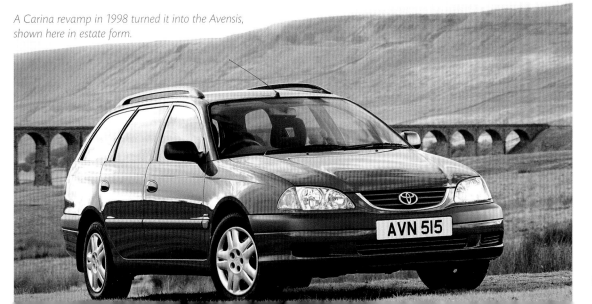

1990s DREAM CARS

Jaguar's XJ220 supercar was a genuine 213mph machine, but an economic slump in 1991 saw buyers try to wriggle out of their orders.

The automotive world entered the new decade on a glamorous high, with the greatest names in driving excitement jostling to offer the planet's ultimate speed machine. The hysteria was traceable back to 1987 and the visceral, 201mph Ferrari F40 – the world's first standard production car guaranteed to smash through the 200mph barrier. Anxious not to be outshone, in 1991 the mid-engined Jaguar XJ220 supercar was finally ready for delivery to customers, and it was independently proven to be capable of 213mph.

As if that were not hedonistic enough, McLaren's truly awe-inspiring F1 road car was revealed in 1992. Its carbon-fibre chassis, central driving position with two passenger seats set back either side, and 618bhp BMW V12 engine, provided a grand-prix-style driving experience and ultimately the ability to attain 241mph. If you could find a piece of road long and straight enough, that is, and only for the lucky few.

The trouble was, spectacular as these cars were – and we should also include Lamborghini's 1990 Diablo and the 1991 Bugatti EB110 in this exalted company – the world economy juddered into reverse in 1991. In years gone by, limited production supercars such as the F40 and Porsche 959 had commanded a sizeable premium over the list price, and canny speculators had made a killing by selling on the cars they ordered. With the economy tanking, however, these fast-buck merchants tried to wriggle out of their contracts to buy, in particular, the XJ220. This put a sad and premature end to production. Even McLaren struggled to sell 100 F1s and lost a small fortune on each one.

McLaren's awesome F1 of 1993 was the ultimate roadgoing machine of its time, with a central driving position and a 618bhp BMW V12 engine just behind it.

Rarely seen in the UK or anywhere else, as a mere handful were built, the Bugatti EB110GT was another early 1990s supercar killed by the recession.

▲ *Here's one we built earlier: the tight-knit Aston Martin workforce celebrate the 200th example of the handmade Vantage in 1992.*

▼ *The DB7 was to take Aston Martin mainstream in 1993 with a beautiful GT using a few well-disguised Jaguar bits to help keep the cost down.*

It might have been the same for Aston Martin. In 1990 the first few examples of its handmade Virage started to trickle out of the Newport Pagnell factory, soon joined by the brutal 190mph, twin-turbo Vantage edition. But Aston was speeding towards bold new territory. Acquired by Ford in 1990, it was working away on a new, smaller model that used some Jaguar components to make it much more affordable. The supercharged DB7 was unveiled in 1993 to huge acclaim, beginning the process that has made Aston Martin the important worldwide sports-luxury brand it is today.

And Aston was by no means the only carmaker charting new supercar waters. In 1990 Honda shocked the world with its two-seater NSX, a mid-engined stunner that could take on a Ferrari, and yet was as docile and easy to drive in traffic and around town as your mum's Honda Civic. If you fancied indulging yourself then the NSX made a startling alternative to German luxury sports cars like the 1989 Mercedes-Benz SL with its pop-up roll bar, and the 1990 BMW 850i boasting pillarless coupé styling and a 5-litre V12 engine. Both of these would become familiar around the playgrounds of the rich in Monaco and Los Angeles throughout the 1990s; the 1989 Alfa Romeo SZ two-seater coupé, meanwhile, was one for the dedicated enthusiast with its quirky, Zagato-built body, and only 1,036 examples were made, with 287 more open-topped RZ models.

➤ BMW's 850i, with V12 engine, looked slick by any standards but none was quite as distinctive as this one painted by the legendary David Hockney.

˅ Honda's NSX was as easy to drive as an Accord but this mid-engined beauty could mix it with Ferraris when pressured.

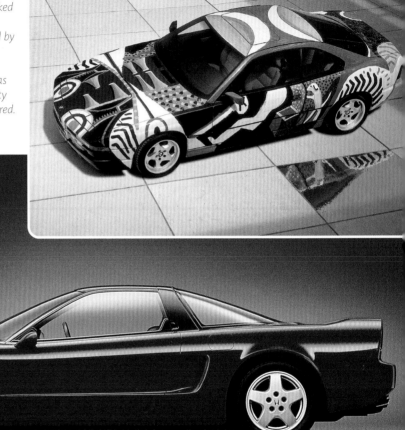

For many people, this super-refined Mercedes-Benz SL, on sale in the UK from 1990, was everything an indulgent sports car needed to be.

The Alfa Romeo SZ was a highly exclusive and rather idiosyncratic Italian thoroughbred with its 3-litre V6 and Zagato-built bodywork.

Of course, many drivers dreamed of owning either a Porsche or a Ferrari in the 1990s, just as in any other decade since 1950. The 964-series 911 had arrived in 1989, giving way to the even smoother-looking 993 series in 1994, which came with all-new multi-link rear suspension. This 911, whether turbocharged or normally aspirated, fastback or soft-top, has turned out to be one of the most desirable 911s in the model's very long history. That's because, in 1998, the incoming 996 series dispensed with the air-cooled engines that had been synonymous with all 911s since 1963. It was claimed they had to switch to conventional water cooling to boost performance and economy and to cut emissions, but for many 911 addicts it was a heresy. Nevertheless, that didn't stop the 996 from being incredibly popular with buyers globally, perhaps proving the diehards wrong.

Over at Ferrari, the 'affordable' mid-engined V8 two-seater 348 was usurped by the F355 in 1994, which was a heavily revised version both inside and out of the previous car. Rather more shocking in 1995 was the replacement for the Testarossa/512TR, the 550 Maranello, which saw a two-seater sports car with a front-mounted V12 engine return to the hallowed Ferrari line-up for the first time since the 365 GTB/4 Daytona of twenty-three years previously. Sharing some parts with the four-seater 456GT, it was a beautiful car for very rich, grown-up people. Meanwhile, the Ferrari F50 of the same year was a dramatic open roadster of which a mere 349 examples were produced to salute Ferrari's fiftieth anniversary.

Bridging the gap between supercar and luxury saloon was the phenomenal Vauxhall Lotus Carlton of 1990, a twin-turbo super-saloon made in limited numbers. Its remarkable grip, 5sec 0–60mph acceleration and 175mph top speed made it like nothing else, and the car gained a notorious reputation when one was stolen and then used as a getaway car in repeated late-night ram-raids.

The Type 964 Porsche 911 in all its glory, captured in 1990; marque aficionados consider these to be some of the finest cars the company ever produced.

The F355 was, believe it or not, the 'entry-level' Ferrari, yet it was high on most automotive wish lists for its exciting performance and gorgeous looks.

◄ A Ferrari for grown-ups – wealthy grown-ups; there was a V12 engine under that long bonnet and there could be no more exciting way to cover huge daily distances in speed and style.

▼ This is the Ferrari F50, new for 1995 and created to celebrate the Italian marque's golden jubilee.

Catch me if you can: once Lotus had had its twin-turbocharged way with the Vauxhall Carlton, it became the getaway car of gangland folklore.

◄ Huge, imposing and double-glazed, the new S-Class arrived in 1991 to reinforce the Mercedes-Benz dominance of the European luxury car sector.

▲ Toyota designed the Lexus LS400 to be more than a match for Jaguar and Mercedes, with exemplary silence, quality and sumptuousness.

A more serene vision of opulence came from Toyota's newly created premium brand Lexus. Its LS400 luxury saloon, launched in 1989, set fastidious new standards of refinement for rivals like Mercedes-Benz and Jaguar to beat. In 1991, Merc's response was the colossal new S-Class, complete with double-glazed side windows to keep the racket of the outside world at bay. Meanwhile Jaguar came up with its traditionally styled XJ8 in 1994 and two years later took the wraps off its XK8, the sumptuous coupé-and-convertible replacement for the venerable XJS range.

▲ Get in: football superstar Michael Owen poses with his brand new XK8 outside Jaguar's Coventry factory in 1996.

The urbane and exclusive Bentley Continental R was the natural choice of the super-rich, and one of the fastest four-seaters they could buy.

With a launch in 1998, the Silver Seraph updated the Rolls-Royce image,
but sported a BMW engine to the consternation of traditionalists.

Perhaps the most elegant luxury machines built during the 1990s still hailed from Britain. The 1991 Bentley Continental R was a super-exclusive, £180,000 grand tourer with old-school charm, and then the Rolls-Royce Silver Seraph/Bentley Arnage range of 1998 was an all-new line-up of traditional four-door limousines, with power now coming from (whisper it) BMW-sourced engines.

If, however, you wanted to throw discretion to the wind and make an unashamed display of your-self, then Chrysler had the answer. It plundered the history books to bring out a modern-day version of the AC Cobra with its 1992 Dodge Viper, a mon-strous sports car with an 8-litre engine in what was then a unique V10 configuration. And five years later it added the Plymouth Prowler, a production-line hot-rod two-seater resembling the sort of roadster that had made California the custom car centre of the world in the 1950s and '60s; no one saw that left-fielder coming ...

↗ *Snake's alive again: the Dodge Viper was a brutally fast and powerful sports car conceived as the latter-day heir to the fabled Shelby/AC Cobra.*

◄ *Were designers at Chrysler fans of the movie* Grease? *Their Plymouth Prowler certainly looked like it had driven straight off the set of a Californian teen romcom.*

VOLVO 850, 1992 & SAAB 900, 1993

Brand-new cars from Sweden don't come along that often but in the early 1990s both Volvo and Saab unveiled their offerings in the medium-sized executive-car sector. They made a fascinating contrast.

Volvo had been working on its 850 since as far back as 1978, fretting on how best to replace its classic 240 – the epitome, in estate form, of the solid Swedish car. In the end, they went out on quite a limb, breaking new ground with an in-line five-cylinder mounted transversely across the front of the boxy-looking saloon and (from 1993) estate, and driving the front wheels. It also had a Delta-link rear suspension system that provided passive rear-wheel steering – giving the car excellent handling – and, in the great tradition of Volvo safety innovations, self-adjusting front seatbelts. It was great to drive in either 2.0- or 2.5-litre form, rapid, secure and with wonderfully supportive seating.

The 850's all-new power unit was unique for a five-cylinder in being mounted transversely.

WHAT THEY SAID AT THE TIME

'The handling has poise and fluency. The 2.5-litre engine is gutsy. B we would still go for the 2-litre GLT and save the money. It's 95% good as the 2.5-litre version.'

Autocar & Motor magazine in November 1992 on the £22,070 85 2.5 GLT.

'The body styling, cabin and tunnel-mounted ignition switch … th new 900 is still a pukka Saab, despite its Cavalier underpinnings. As driver's car, the 900 2.3i is no match for the [BMW] 320i.'

Autocar & Motor magazine in August 1993 on the £17,495 900 2.3

◄ *Volvo traditionalists were glad for the cavernous new 850 estate*

The new 900, meanwhile, felt to Saab fans to be a more compromised car, as it shared its platform and running gear with the front-wheel drive Vauxhall Cavalier; although Saab's own four-cylinder engines were offered, a V6 model also used a General Motors (GM) engine, diluting the Saab individualism further. GM had become a major shareholder, and so had the whip hand.

However, there were convertible and turbocharged models, and Saab itself worked overtime to make sure these highly capable cars reflected the Swedes' engineering and safety philosophy. One unique feature was the 'Night Panel', the facility to shut off every dashboard light source except the speedometer, to remove distractions and aid nocturnal driving concentration ...

Both made characterful, high-quality alternatives to BMWs and Mercedes-Benzes throughout the 1990s. By the decade's end, the Volvo had been renamed the S70 and the Saab the 9-3.

This 900 SE five-door ran the smooth V6 engine also found in many top Vauxhalls.

Two-door convertible and coupé versions of the Saab 900.

WHO LOVED THEM?

Not every executive car buyer appreciated the overt sportiness or chrome-encrusted bling of German offerings, nor the plebeian prestige of big Fords and Rovers. Plus, both Volvo and Saab continued to set the pace with safety features, which made them the choice of the thinking man or woman who still craved enjoyment and style in their drives.

CITROËN XANTIA, 1993

Devotees of the Citroën marque tended to demand advanced, interesting design, which is one reason why there was a rather chilly reception to the ZX as it partly replaced the Citroën BX. Now the Xantia was here to take over from the larger-engined BXs, and with its hydro-pneumatic suspension system, here was a natural heir at last to Citroën's traditions of exceptional ride quality.

The Hydractive II system on larger-engined models was computer controlled to give serene coverage of road bumps, moving to tautness in fast cornering, and allied to a pre-programmed steering rear axle.

That, however, was just the start. From 1994 the Xantia Activa offered an 'active' suspension system with special anti-roll bars, hydraulic cylinders and complex computer co-ordination that all but eradicated body roll in corners. In handling tests designed to avoid a stray animal encountered around a corner, the Activa even today has been found to out-swerve a modern supercar. Its roadholding was quite simply amazing.

Only problem was that the Activa was naturally much more expensive than equivalent rivals thanks to its technology. Buyers were thin on the ground and, indeed, when the Xantia became obsolete in 2002, Citroën elected to abandon its fluid-based suspension system for good.

This is the Activa version of Citroën's Xantia that can still, today, run rings around supercars.

WHAT THEY SAID AT THE TIME

'Hydractive II suspension is what sets the VSX apart from the £2000 cheaper SX, and it repays the investment handsomely. It corners fast and flat and dismisses broken blacktop, but it also provides tactile information about the road surface entirely missing from the lesser model.'

Autocar & Motor magazine in September 1993 on the £15,995 Xantia 1.9 TD VSX.

WHO LOVED IT?

In one way, Citroën had reached the limits of what people would pay for futuristic technology; the Activa was an expensive flop despite its astonishing tarmac-gripping capabilities. The range as a whole, though, proved popular, with 1.2m Xantias sold and a strong following in the UK despite the locals having to get their tongues around the 'Zan-tee-ah' name ...

As to the rest of the car, it was a svelte, Italian-styled (by Bertone) alternative to the Cavalier and Mondeo, supplied as a five-door hatchback or estate. A wide spectrum of engine sizes covered 1.6 to 2 litres in petrol and 1.9–2.1 litres as turbodiesels; the 1.9 TD was the bestseller although many British buyers chose the 2-litre petrol, while from 1997 there was also a 3-litre V6 in a highly refined luxury edition.

▲ The 1998 model-year Xantia had a frontal refresh to keep its Bertone lines desirable.

➤ Xantia estate, in this case the 1.9 TD LX, helped the French onslaught against the Mondeo.

FIAT PUNTO, 1993, PLUS BARCHETTA & COUPÉ

The Punto had the unenviable task of replacing one of the most popular cars of all time: the Fiat Uno. And pitched into a market already saturated with truly excellent supermini choices from Ford, Nissan and Renault, there was some extraordinarily tough competition.

▲ *There was lots of room and great visibility in the Punto; this is an 85 ELX five-door.*

Fortunately, not only was the Punto attractive thanks to its appealing Giugiaro styling, but it was also exceptionally spacious front and back, well packaged and – maybe the key factor – keenly priced. The ride quality and heavy steering (without power-assistance) were not the best, but the driving position and all-round visibility made it tops for a mix of long-distance and city motoring.

All Puntos shared the same all-independent suspension, and engines ranged from 1.1 to 1.6 petrol, including a 1.4 Turbo plus a 1.7-litre diesel option too. Yet as to the fun options reflecting typical Italian flair, the Punto offered more than most.

◄ *The pretty Punto-based Barchetta (it means 'little boat') was only available with left-hand drive, even in the UK.*

◄ *Temple of dune: the soft-top Punto offered budget open-air fun.*

You could have a six-speed gearbox with the smallest engine; then there was a feisty Sporting edition, and a sizzling GT with up to 134bhp. Fiat went even further, offering a neat Cabriolet with an electrically powered soft top. In 1994 it added a Punto-based sports car to its range in the form of the gorgeous little Barchetta, which did come to the UK albeit in left-hand drive form only. On top of that, there was also the Fiat Coupé. Its idiosyncratic Pininfarina styling was like nothing else available, and the turbocharged version of the 16-valve 2-litre engine made it a miniature Ferrari, with a 140mph top speed and 0–60mph in 6.8sec. These 1990s Fiats were bursting with spirit, giving them a character lacking from many more efficient competitors.

▼ *Fiat's Coupé had unique, sharp-edged styling and excellent performance.*

HO LOVED IT?

eap, easy to live with and generally great fun to drive,
 Punto found plenty of friends. It was one of the
 cars of the London Motorfair in October 1993. Fiat
oyed a sales explosion with this new small hatchback.
ld quality was good rather than exceptional and that,
ed to low list prices, tended to see used values slide
er than for equivalents, making a second-hand Punto
entially quite a bargain.

MERCEDES-BENZ C-CLASS, 1993

In 1993 the so-called 'entry-level' Merc was still quite a large car; a fastidiously constructed alternative to the Vauxhall Cavalier for those who could stump up the substantial price to enjoy the privilege.

There was nothing to frighten the horses in the C-Class's sober and conservative outer design, despite the careful attention given to aerodynamics. Likewise, the interior was a paragon of good taste, with superb seats and excellent ergonomics. On every level, this was a car to be proud of, although there was a marked difference in smoothness and responses between the four-cylinder engines (1.8- to 2.3-litre petrol and 2.0- to 2.2-litre diesel) and the 2.8-litre straight-six. There was also a five-cylinder diesel with or without turbocharger; in 1997, an efficiency rethink saw the diesel engines switch to a common-rail design and a V6 replace the straight-six to cut emissions while maintaining decent performance levels. At the same time came a new five-speed automatic transmission.

∧ *If you could afford it then a Mercedes-Benz C-Class Esprit was probably the best medium-sized saloon available.*

◄ *The C-Class estate was highly practical, although a bit too ritzy for runs to the tip ...*

In natural comparisons with BMW 3 Series cars, the Mercedes was generally found to be less sharply sporting, and in an attempt to close that gap Mercedes created the C230 Kompressor in 1997, featuring a supercharged 2.3-litre engine shared with the later SLK sports car, and 190bhp in store. It was the first supercharger Merc had offered since the 1930s. In 1996, though, came a C-Class supercar in the shape of the C36 AMG, with race-tuned suspension and a hand-built 3.6-litre V6 pumping out 276bhp. It could hit 60mph from standstill in 5.8sec and its true 169mph top speed was artificially restricted to 155mph. For 1998, even this hot rod was bettered by the C43 AMG, packing a 4.3-litre V8 with a fearsome 306bhp and a meaty 303lb ft of torque (pulling power). AMG, by the way, was a race-tuning company Mercedes took over entirely in 1998.

In spite of all the focus on power and prestige, the practical C-Class estate introduced in 1996 quickly accounted for a large proportion of the cars sold until 2000.

WHO LOVED IT?

Building on the solid success of the 190 models that preceded it, the C-Class was designed to appeal to the core Mercedes-Benz demographic: well-heeled people whether in business or not. Apart from its prestige credentials, it was – as for the 190 – once again in high demand as a taxi across European cities. And it was a phenomenally good seller; with 1.8 million examples sold it was, for instance, hugely more successful (and profitable) than the Citroën Xantia on p.70.

The AMG-tuned C43 packed a 4.3-litre V8 under its gleaming bonnet.

PEUGEOT 306, 1993

Peugeot was a pioneer of 'platform sharing'. It's the crafty business of creating several different cars from a single rolling chassis/floorpan/wheelbase, saving a king's ransom in development costs. At first, the practice was used to quickly create new models, such as the Citroën LN, Citroën Visa and Talbot Samba from the Peugeot 104 after 1970s takeovers of other car companies; soon Peugeots and Citroëns were being planned from the start to use the same mechanical platforms – steering, suspension and weight distribution included.

For the stylish new 306, the timings had gone a bit awry. Under those sophisticated-looking Pininfarina lines was the barely different Citroën ZX of two years earlier. Consequently, the two cars offered near-identical dynamics and engine choices, with contemporary observers feeling that, if anything, the Citroën had the slight edge for the all-important balance between comfortable travel and front-wheel-drive road manners that were safe and responsive enough to appeal to owners who actually enjoyed driving, rather than just trundling from points A to B.

For all the equivalence, the 306 offered more choice. A year after its 1993 introduction Peugeot unveiled a four-door sedan iteration together with a very desirable four-seater cabriolet that could also be ordered

With a six-speed gearbox, the 306 GTi-6 saw sales among enthusiasts really take off.

WHAT THEY SAID AT THE TIME

'The Peugeot 306 XRdt is simply the best affordable turbodiesel you can buy. You have the potential to cover almost double the amount of miles you would in a comparable petrol 306, without sacrificing any of the performance. The Citroën ZX is cheaper. There, it's not perfect.'

Autocar & Motor magazine in September 1993 on the £12,000 306 1.9 XRdt.

HO LOVED IT?

this hotly contested market sector, the 306 could ld its head up as one of the very best, with its diesel gines notable for especially lusty performance and cellent economy. The 306 would indeed prove to be e epitome of popular, Pininfarina-penned Peugeots th exemplary chassis design.

with a hardtop for cold winters. The customary mid-life refresh in 1997 ushered in a neat 306 estate too.

One more difference from the ZX: the 306 was made in Britain. Or, at least, assembled here, at Peugeot's Ryton-on-Dunsmore plant just outside Coventry. It was from there that a particularly coveted version originated, the sporty 306 Rallye, based on the 167bhp GTi-6 with its six-speed gearbox. A mere 500 of these performance machines were produced.

◄ *The estate version made a much more stylish alternative to an Escort or Astra.*

↗ *The neat 306 dashboard was part of the handsome Pininfarina styling.*

▼ *The gorgeous 306 cabriolet enjoyed notably sleek lines with its canvas top folded neatly away.*

ROVER 600, 1993 & HONDA ACCORD, 1993

The Rover 600 was a very good car, as well it ought to have been since it was really the 1993 Honda Accord with some different panels and a Trad Brit interior clad, in some models, in leather and embellished with wood veneer.

Even then, though, the base car was not quite the Accord the rest of the world knew but the European model built in Swindon, Wiltshire, which was derived from the Ascot Innova from the Far East. This Ascot and the 600 were developed side-by-side in Japan as part of the ongoing Rover–Honda working partnership – really a joint venture that helped Rover generate new cars on the cheap.

Nevertheless, the 600 was mostly unique from an external perspective, with only the windscreen, front doors, lower rear doors and roof identical to the Accord/Ascot. The distinctive Rover did without the Honda's third side window and the rest had a slightly retro feeling. The 30-year-old designer Richard Woolley drew on motifs from classic Rovers like the P4 of the 1950s, with a prominent chrome grille upfront and matching number-plate surround at the back. Inside, a broad centre console and chrome kickplates in the door sills were among the clever ways of disguising the Honda-derived dashboard and architecture. The main engine choice was a four-cylinder Honda unit of 1.8-, 2.0- or 2.3-litre sizes, although Rover did sneak its own turbocharged 2-litre twin-cam into the sporty 620Ti, and all the turbodiesels used Rover's 2-litre L-series unit.

WHAT THEY SAID AT THE TIME

'From the way its suspension filters out road noise to the way its body sealing deadens any wind roar, the Rover is as quiet as you could hope. Its friendly chassis makes is a fine companion for enjoying demanding backroads.'

Autocar & Motor magazine in April 1993 on the £14,995 620 Si.

Largely the same car as the Rover 600, the Accord was built in Honda's new Swindon factory.

Interior of the 618: the centre console was another facet unique to Rover.

Rover designers worked wonders to give the 600 its distinctiveness; this is the range-topping 623.

L623 EYN

HO LOVED IT?

600 was a car giving the best of two motoring worlds
e excellence and reliability of a Honda mixed with
character and design flourishes that once defined
y British saloons. With over 270,000 examples
, it received a warm reception from both private
orists and fleet buyers, and easily outsold its Honda
ning mate built down the road in Swindon.

The 600 was intended to take over from the unlovely Austin Montego and was built at Rover's Cowley plant. Throughout the 1990s it gave Rover a more than credible contender in the all-important medium-sized saloon class.

SUBARU IMPREZA/IMPREZA TURBO, 1994

In the short lifespan of this one model, a relatively small car manufacturer was transformed from worthy provider of farmers' estate cars to worldwide totem of unstoppable high-performance driving. With British rallying know-how, and star European drivers, the Impreza Turbo grabbed second place in its first-ever rally in 1993, scooping its first event victory in 1994, and going on to clinch the Manufacturers' Championship title for three years on the trot, 1995–97.

The compact Impreza range had arrived in March 1992 and the car was on sale widely by November. It was all-new with the EJ series 'boxer' (flat four-cylinder) 1.6- to 2-litre engine range from the larger Legacy, with their exceptional mechanical balance and low centre of gravity.

Top of the range by 1994 was the 2000 Turbo AWD (known as the WRX in Japan) with four-wheel drive and 208bhp on tap (already 4bhp more than the hallowed Ford Sierra Cosworth). A full body kit featured gigantic, circular driving lights at the front and an aerofoil on the boot, while the bonnet sported a prominent air scoop.

Prodrive, the Banbury-based British company running the Subaru World Rally Team, could see that here was a real contender. Its speed and tautness were obvious

from the start, and they were campaigned throughout the 1990s, latterly in evolution STI form. It helped Colin McRae become the first Brit ever to achieve world rally champion status, and Subaru UK issued 200 limited edition examples called, of course, the Series McRae. A completely new Impreza was released in 2000.

It looked innocent enough, but the turbocharged, all-wheel drive Impreza was an astonishing performer.

Colin McRae with the limited-edition Impreza carrying the late rally driver's heroic name.

WHO LOVED IT?

Fast car fanatics, whether they could afford an Impreza Turbo or not, were in awe of this rally-conquering saloon. The turbocharged, four-wheel drive Impreza became the world's most desirable sports saloon in very short order, creating a tin-top motor sport legend ranked alongside the Mini Cooper, Ford Escort or Audi Quattro.

WHAT THEY SAID AT THE TIME

'Wow. Unbelievable. Those were about the only words we could spit out after launching Subaru's unlikely supercar to 60mph in just 5.8sec. Just for the record, that's faster than a Delta Integrale or an Escort Cosworth. Or a Porsche 968. When the power does come in, it is handed out to the wheels with the most grip, giving the little Subaru truly amazing wet weather grip.'

Autocar magazine in April 1994 on the £17,499 Impreza 2000 Turbo AWD.

As well as the saloon, Subaru offered this not-quite-an-estate five-door – superb in wintry weather.

VAUXHALL CORSA MKI, 1993 & OMEGA, 1993

April 1993 saw the Nova replaced after a highly successful ten-year stint as Vauxhall's supermini. Just like the outgoing model, though, the all-new Corsa hailed from neither of Vauxhall's UK plants at Luton or Ellesmere Port, Cheshire, but from General Motors' Spanish factory.

Most of the power units were familiar from the Nova, dependable four-cylinder units in 1.2-, 1.4- and 1.6-litre sizes, with five-speed gearboxes attached to all but the weediest engine. For the GSi performance version, Lotus worked over the 107bhp engine, giving it a 16-valve cylinder head that produced a sparkling performer: 0–60mph in 8.7sec and a top whack of 118mph.

But just as remarkable in a different way was the 1.5 turbo-diesel in the TD model that gave 47mpg on average but – thanks to the turbo boost – performance that fair snapped at the GSI's wide rubber heels.

In 1997, a mid-life refresh also ushered in a super-economy 1-litre, three-cylinder engine, and more help from Lotus in tuning the suspension and steering to sharpen up every Corsa's responses.

WHO LOVED IT?

Vauxhall made a huge impact with its opening advertising campaign for the Corsa, hiring supermodels like Naomi Campbell and Linda Evangelista, Christy Turlington and Kate Moss to do revengeful battle with its own 'super model' (the Campaign Against Pornography slammed these ads as a 'fantasy of bondage, torture and sado-masochism'). In truth, the stylish Corsa was always a laggard in class standards, but that was no barrier to huge UK sales and a residency in the bestsellers list for the whole of the '90s.

Naomi Campbell in a scene from the Corsa TV ad that caused such a fuss.

Three-door Corsa Sport: a good-looking supermini but never rated highly for its dynamics.

The Vauxhall Omega was one of Europe's last non-premium-badged executive cars.

The Corsa's harmonious, smoothly rounded shape stood out immediately with either three or five doors. Unlike for the Nova, there were no conventional saloon editions (although these were later produced for Brazilian and Chinese markets). However, the Combo van, with a Corsa front end grafted on to a cargo-hungry metal box at the back, proved very popular, while Britain's dog-groomers, florists and cleaning companies could opt for the car-like Corsavan, a utility three-door with its rear side windows and back seats missing.

Another Vauxhall new for 1993 was the Omega, a replacement for the Carlton which, just as for the Corsa, was a Vauxhall-badged import from Opel (in Germany) for buyers of large executive cars, of which it was a solid exponent if a big, rear-drive saloon or estate was what you wanted.

JAGUAR XJ, 1994

The first supercharged six-cylinder engine in a mass-produced car was the proud boast of this big new Jaguar executive saloon. It was designed in secret under the codename of X300, and was the first model from the marque to be totally overseen by Ford, which had taken control at Jaguar in 1990 after paying £1.6bn to acquire this world-famous British marque.

The XJR was an astounding large sports saloon, into whose 4-litre straight six the supercharger pumped extra air for added engine power. It could roar to 60mph from standstill in 5.7sec, and 100mph in 15sec. Top speed was limited to 155mph. And all this in sumptuous luxury, albeit in a cabin somewhat cosy for such a large car. Other engines on offer included a 3.2-litre six offering excellent value for £17,000 less, and a 6-litre V12 that could reach 155mph in silken silence.

▲ *With the V12-engined XJ12 on the right, this is Jaguar's XJ range in 1994.*

▼ *The supercharged engine endowed the slingshot XJR with wondrous overtaking ability.*

WHAT THEY SAID AT THE TIME

'The best riding and handling Jaguar to date but also the best-assembled car yet to roll out of Browns Lane. The supercharged engine's monstrous mid-range torque endows the XJR with wondrous overtaking ability.'

Autocar magazine in September 1994 on the £45,450 XJR.

▲ This new XJ's cabin was just as you'd expect, a soothing cocoon of leather and walnut.

▼ Jaguar's AJ6 engine was the mainstay of the range – great to see that traditional, on-board toolkit!

WHO LOVED IT?

Jaguar's thorough makeover of its staple XJ luxury saloon had taken heed of what its biggest fans wanted, and that was a return to elegant curves and a characterful ownership experience. It was setting out a stall very different to alternatives from Mercedes-Benz, BMW and Lexus. In some ways, it rather froze Jaguar's evolution in the 1990s, but for now the new XJ was applauded everywhere as Jaguar back on form.

This new XJ reinstated the four-round-headlamp frontage of the original XJ for the whole range, with a sculpted bonnet to match. Indeed, the well-loved profile of the XJ had been smoothed and tapered to make this new saloon look very swish indeed.

However, within a mere three years there were more major changes. The entire engine range was superseded by the brand new AJ-V8 in a line-up using the XJ8 title in place of the familiar XJ6 and XJ12. It came in 3.2- and 4-litre forms, and again including a 4-litre supercharged edition. There was even more emphasis on roundedness inside and out, with the jarringly oblong instrument pod now jettisoned for circular dials set into the gleaming walnut veneer of the dashboard. A total transition to luxury was complete with a switch to five-speed automatic transmission as the only option, the sporty supercharged XJR included.

RANGE ROVER MKII, 1994

Land Rover conducted detailed market research among its customers, and mostly it found they loved their Range Rovers just as they were. Hence, a conservative approach shaped a new one. That, and a tight £300m budget, which forced engineers to make the new Rangie, in effect, a re-body of the long-wheelbase 'Classic' LSE.

Arguably, the iconic character was diluted by, for instance, changing the round headlamps to oblong ones, but the new Range Rover was significantly more aerodynamic, so improved noise suppression and fuel economy were excellent gains. Inside, an entirely new dash was a giant step up in fit and finish, with a particularly stylish, curved centre console.

Technically, the car adopted the LSE's electronic air-suspension system across the range, incorporated into an 18 per cent stiffer ladder-frame chassis, with standard anti-lock brakes. The five suspension heights available, lowest to highest, spoke for themselves: Access, Motorway, Standard, Off-Road and Off-Road Extended. It remained pretty much unrivalled in its relentless off-road ability, the same as its famous forebear.

The venerable Rover V8 thundered on, now in 190bhp 4.0- and 225bhp 4.6-litre sizes; there was also a BMW-supplied 2.5-litre turbodiesel. They all benefited

Mud-plugging aristocracy – the new Range Rover was still the off-road king.

WHAT THEY SAID AT THE TIME

'The king-of-the-hill 4.6 HSE, quite apart from demolishing the contemporary opposition — Cherokee, Shogun, Landcruiser — presents a cast-iron case as a luxury car alternative; it sponges away whatever the road surface throws at it.'

Autocar magazine in October 1994 on the £43,950 4.6 HSE.

Inside a 4.6-litre HSE, where the all-new dashboard was a radical departure for Range Rover drivers.

WHO LOVED IT?

It sold strongly, and 167,041 found buyers. However, they were often frustrated by the unreliability of the more complex electronics and sometimes the overall build quality. With BMW in charge, this was simply unacceptable, and much effort was poured into improving standards at the Solihull factory. On this basis, the second-generation Range Rover was soon regarded as an interim model so that BMW could oversee a totally new, third-generation car from scratch.

from BMW/Bosch engine-management systems. Transmission choice included five-speed manual and four-speed automatic.

The Autobiography personalisation programme was introduced in 1995 for the 4.0 SE and 4.6 HSE, with inexhaustible combinations of non-standard paintwork, leather upholstery and wood trim. A year later the choice extended to a vast roster of in-car entertainment options and then, in 1997, the first satellite-navigation system. From September 1998 there was regularly a Vogue SE edition among the line-up, groaning with equipment, and the final one cost an eye-popping £57,995 complete with its integral TV and video package.

A ghosted image of the new car shows a familiar chassis with a new air-suspension system.

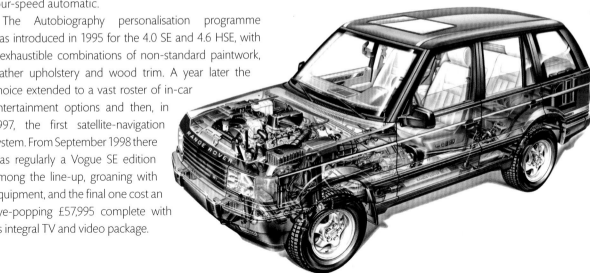

1990s
CAR CULTURE

No one had coined the term 'petrolheads' yet, but some 5 million so-inclined, car-obsessed viewers regularly tuned into *Top Gear* on BBC2, making it the top-watched TV programme on the channel most weeks. At the start of the 1990s it was still a general-interest motoring magazine show anchored by William Woollard but in 1991 he was usurped by former second-hand car dealer Quentin Willson. Starting in 1988, magazine columnist Jeremy Clarkson was also a regular face, with increasingly strident views as his notoriety grew. In 1995, for example, his acerbic assessment of the admittedly mundane new Vauxhall Vectra as nothing but 'a box on wheels' caused a huge furore in the car industry; remember, this was very much in the pre-internet age, and for many *Top Gear* was the oracle. It was only as the influence of the worldwide web started to grow at the close of the decade that the show's influence wilted.

▲ Every issue of Max Power *magazine was an orgy of speed, horsepower and lurid customisation – just what its car-crazy young readers wanted, in fact.*

▼ *Motormouth: Jeremy Clarkson wielded huge influence as one of the BBC's* Top Gear *presenters; he liked this Jag but was none too keen on the Vauxhall Vectra.*

Car magazines, of course, were also a vital source of information for consumers and enthusiasts, and *Top Gear* itself launched a monthly newsstand spin-off in 1993. It was pitched straight into battle with *Autocar & Motor*, an amalgam of Britain's two oldest weeklies. It was quite an achievement when the magazine, reverting to plain *Autocar*, celebrated its centenary in 1995, shortly after it had published its 5,000th full and forensic road test.

But the new bad boy on the block was the monthly *Max Power*, a raucous journal crammed with tuned cars, scantily clad girls and reports on street cruises, high-speed antics and tyre-smoking burnouts. It was perfectly calculated to enrage caravanners, police chiefs and, indeed, concerned parents. But, as a kickback on the tedious prevailing atmosphere of speed curbing, safety advances and emissions reduction, it hit the spot spectacularly. It was the laddish car equivalent to the equally brash *Loaded*. Not long after its launch in 1993 it was Europe's biggest-circulation car magazine, selling almost 240,000 copies. But by 2010 when it closed, circulation was a tenth of this peak.

A decidedly clunky looking web page hosted by early-adopter Fiat to promote its Bravo in the mid 1990s; we were on the cusp of the internet explosion.

For those seeking a gentler, more elegant – but still exciting – motoring environment, the first Goodwood Festival of Speed of 1993 was a watershed – a glorious celebration of speed and fun featuring everything from bicycles to supersonic jets, and fast cars of all types. At its core was a hill-climb course on Lord March's Chichester estate, which competitors were encouraged to enjoy. A massive social event, by 2003 it was attracting more spectators than the annual British Grand Prix, and after the demise of any 'official' British motor show, the Goodwood Festival stepped in as probably the best-attended general car show.

Nostalgia, indeed, was becoming big business. In 1993, Rover and the British Motor Industry Heritage Trust opened a mightily impressive £8m Heritage Centre museum at Gaydon, Warwickshire, to showcase its rich and varied past. And three years later, the government sprang a surprise by exempting all veteran, vintage and classic cars registered before 1 January 1973 – most lovingly preserved by their owners as part of the country's heritage – from Vehicle Excise Duty, or road tax as most older people still called it. Yet with classic car

values rocketing once again after their late 1980s crash, this was fertile ground for skulduggery. Sadly, it now seemed, in the classic car world 'silver-spooned' could sometimes mean 'cunningly silver-tongued', as aristocrat Lord Brocket – along with two of his underlings – broke up and hid precious Ferraris and Maseratis in a bungled insurance con in 1996, for which milord did time in stir.

Buying second-hand cars was set to change dramatically as eBay went live in 1995. This and other online marketplaces gradually sucked the life out of printed classified ads, making combing through *Exchange & Mart* and the local rag things of the past. People with more money than sense still abounded, though: in December 1993 the world record price for a registration number was crushed when a nightclub owner splashed £203,500 for the right to sport K1 NGS on his car. And there was even something exciting for those not actually owning a car of their own, as London saw the all-new TX1 purpose-built taxi enter service in 1997, ending an almost forty-year reign of the ubiquitous FX4 Fairway.

Held in the grounds of Lord March's Goodwood country seat, with a great hill-climb course on hand, the first Festival of Speed proved a huge and lasting success.

In 1993, the British Motor Heritage Centre opened at Gaydon, a temple to great British cars of the past. Talking of which, the cherished 1969 MGB you see outside it enjoyed road-tax-free status after a rule change in 1996.

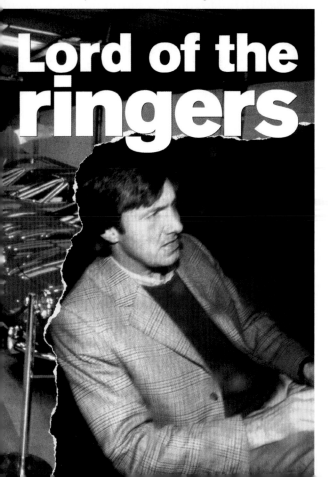

Lord of the ringers

In 1996 the Society of Motor Manufacturers & Traders celebrated the British motor industry's centenary – it was 100 years since the first Daimler was built in Coventry. Yet in 1994 the very ethos of a mainstream British-owned motor industry was in question; British Aerospace announced that it would sell off Rover Group – which included most of the famous names from the past – and the buyer was BMW. By 2000, the same German company had acquired Rolls-Royce, with Bentley picked off by Volkswagen.

The most shocking car crash of the decade was undoubtedly the 1997 Paris accident that killed Princess Diana, along with her companion Dodi Fayed. But it was by no means the only celebrity car death to make the headlines. Film director Alan J. Pakula was killed in his Volvo in New York in November 1999 and, just a month later, actor Desmond Llewellyn – Q in the Bond movies – died in a collision in his Renault Megane.

Cars and criminality was a recurring theme of the 1990s. In 1991 the craze for 'hotting' made the news, with cars being hot-wired and stolen to perform dangerous driving displays in empty car parks. Then, in 1992, thousands of young people began using the ease of access offered by the M25 to turn up at illegal raves all over the Home Counties, their sheer numbers often overwhelming police efforts to close down the dance parties in open fields or abandoned buildings. In 1995

'airbagging' was the new menace, with joyriders deliberately crashing cars to trigger their airbags for some pointlessly dangerous kicks. And, let's face it, there were ever more to inflate with Volvo introducing side-impact airbags in 1994, Kia bringing in the world's first knee airbag in its Sportage in 1996, Audi adding the first six-airbag system in '97 and the BMW 7 Series offering the first side head airbags in '98.

‹ A national icon refreshed: the new LTI (for London Taxis International) TX1 would soon become the capital's most familiar 'car'.

‹ All right, sonny, you're nicked, and quite possibly for having 'hotted' this here 1998 SEAT Leon.

⋏ Form an orderly Q, 007; actor Desmond Llewellyn, on the left, sadly died in a car crash in 1999 after years of telling James Bond (here Pierce Brosnan) to drive safely.

▲ Seems like a strange way to get your kicks – to the face – but 1990s tearaways were stealing cars and then triggering their airbags for none-too-smart high jinks.

➤ Airbags were sprouting from all sorts of spots within cars as manufacturers competed to fit more and more; this side airbag, for example, was standard kit in the Daihatsu Sirion.

Finally, we should recall the top-selling cars of the whole 1990s – often in two or even three successive versions – and the quantities sold to give an accurate idea of what most British drivers chose as their steeds. And here they are: 1: Ford Fiesta – 1,214,062; 2: Ford Escort – 1,165,231; 3: Vauxhall Astra – 916,714; 4: Ford Mondeo – 718,720; 5: Rover 200 – 660,605; 6: Vauxhall Cavalier – 634,917; 7: Vauxhall Corsa – 520,976; 8: Volkswagen Golf – 437,155; 9: Nissan Micra – 422,644; and 10: Renault Clio – 414,964. As for the 1980s, cars with British badges still prevailed but, while the Mondeo and Corsa were imported, the Micra was homegrown. Meanwhile, both the Golf and Clio were good examples of how, in the European single market, attractive foreign models became true fixtures of the British roadscape.

Registering an interest: three Vauxhall models were among the bestselling cars for the whole decade, keeping the dealer network super-busy.

TOYOTA RAV4, 1994

▲ *This RAV4 was a true breakthrough, offering a car-like experience with SUV ride height.*

It's rare for a Japanese manufacturer to allow the name of an individual designer to be revealed, much less be attached to a particular product. An exception was made for Masakatu Nonaka, the chief engineer and, by the company's own admission, the guiding light behind what became the Recreational Activity Vehicle with four-wheel drive, or RAV4. He joined the company in 1967 and in 1988 he was put in charge of developing a compact sport-utility vehicle (SUV), partly because he loved 4x4s and outdoor hobbies like mountain- and trials-biking. His research included a long trip to Europe to see how off-roaders were being used as everyday cars in towns and cities.

▼ *The drop-down soft top on some RAV4s turned them into open-air fun cars.*

WHAT THEY SAID AT THE TIME

'Inside, the RAV4 offers a fine driving position and controls that are intelligently laid out. Here is a tall, fat-tyred mudplugger that can actually reach 60mph in a remarkable 10.1sec, and top out at 107mph. Of its breed the RAV4 is the champ, and it's difficult to imagine that changing any time soon.'

Autocar magazine in July 1995 on the £15,945 RAV4 GX five-door.

All of this fed into his design that was actually a pure, monocoque road car, with high ground clearance, large wheels and tyres, and permanent four-wheel drive, rather than something truck-like with a separate chassis.

So the car used structural parts from the Corolla and Carina and power came from a 2-litre, fuel-injected twin-cam engine from the Toyota Camry. The suspension was tuned for great on-road capability but was still robust enough for the odd sojourn off-road – and it was certainly at ease in slippery conditions or on moderately severe terrain. In effect, it was a four-wheel drive road car given the high-up driving position and chunky proportions that SUV buyers craved.

Neat touches included a swing-out rear cargo door with its release handle integrated into the rear lamp cluster, and lift-out aluminium roof panels to create an open car without the need to offer a separate soft-top model.

Toyota also broke its own protocol by making the RAV4 the first new model to receive its world debut in Europe, at the 1994 Geneva Motor Show. A year later and the even more practical five-door model joined it. Great cars, both.

⋏ The cockpit of the RAV4 was conventionally styled, with masses of headroom.

⋎ This five-door estate was the most versatile, with a spare wheel mounted on the back door to maximise cargo space inside.

WHO LOVED IT?

Toyota researchers had discovered that 62 per cent of buyers of existing mini-SUVs in, for example, Germany were trading-in cars like Volkswagen Golfs. So the RAV4 was spot-on in offering all European buyers a brilliant new on-trend product with all the benefits of a four-wheel-drive off-roader, yet none of the drawbacks. Brilliantly built, super-reliable, and great to drive even twenty-five years on.

VAUXHALL TIGRA, 1994

The choice among very small coupés was mostly restricted to uninspiring Japanese cars until the Tigra popped up its perky face. The two-plus-two, with its token pair of rear seats, had been seen first as a design concept car at the 1993 Frankfurt and London motor shows, but the reception was so positive that it was rolling down the Spanish production line just one year later in September 1994.

Although not a single body panel was shared, the Tigra was based wholesale on the running gear of the small Corsa hatchback, and even the dashboard was the same. However, as the Tigra was 150kg heavier, the equivalent three-door Corsa remained very slightly faster.

The smaller 88bhp 1.4-litre engine was the mild option and was the only one offered with a four-speed automatic gearbox (from 1995). The 104bhp 1.6, on the other hand, gave a more vivid account of itself. They were both Ecotec double-overhead-camshaft units with 16 valves and fuel-injection.

Considering its diminutive size, the bigger-engined Tigra was quite the goer, thanks to its excellent aerodynamics and tall gear ratios. It could beat 120mph and hit 60mph from rest in 10.2sec. Although it was easily possible to find other small cars offering a more inspiring

Tigras are getting rare and might die out, like the Seattle Coffee Company did ...

WHO LOVED IT?

When production of the Tigra came to an end in 2001, exactly 256,392 examples had found owners, with a good number of those in the UK. As an easy-to-live-with small coupé for a couple – newlyweds or retired but definitely not with growing kids – it was for a while the default choice. The Corsa underpinnings lent it dependability if not great dynamics.

driving experience, nothing else had the Tigra's fantastic styling. Rivals such as the Honda Civic Coupé and Toyota Paseo didn't even come close for visual impact, and the Tigra in many ways paved the way for the new MINI of 2001 in throwing total practicality to the wind in attempts to give a small car some individuality.

WHAT THEY SAID AT THE TIME

'It grips wells, steers accurately enough, and is reasonably good fun in a slightly hamfisted, old-fashioned way. If you want great looks and a reasonably good drive, go for a Tigra.'

Autocar magazine in March 1996 on the £14,470 Tigra 1.6.

⋏ *Something to shout about: no other small coupé looked as cool as the Tigra.*

➤ *This is the Tigra 1.4 automatic, but it's still urging you to jump in and have fun.*

VOLKSWAGEN POLO, 1994

Here was a new bellwether for quality in small cars. It was a little more costly than its competitors, but the generous equipment levels across the whole range justified that, even before the Polo's excellent driving characteristics and material quality were considered. The cabin was also uncommonly spacious and thoughtfully designed. It was a winner from the off, and soon gathered numerous awards from magazines and organisations to signify that.

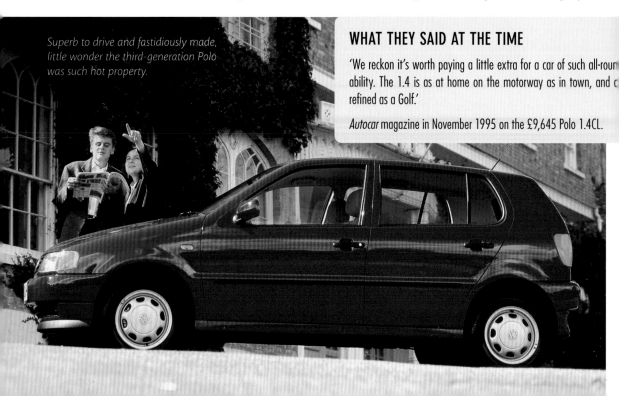

Superb to drive and fastidiously made, little wonder the third-generation Polo was such hot property.

WHAT THEY SAID AT THE TIME

'We reckon it's worth paying a little extra for a car of such all-rour ability. The 1.4 is as at home on the motorway as in town, and c refined as a Golf.'

Autocar magazine in November 1995 on the £9,645 Polo 1.4CL.

The debut of this third-generation Polo was timely; its predecessor had been around for over thirteen years in one form or another. Hence Volkswagen was the last major supermini producer to offer both three- and five-door options. In late 1995 it also caught up belatedly with the industry norm by adding 1.9-litre diesel and turbodiesel engines.

VW adapted the platform of its Golf MkIII to the new Polo, which meant most of the drivetrain was identical. Not only did that mean a masterful compromise between ride quality and handling but also an exceptional standard of mechanical refinement. The 1-litre engine was strictly for around-town economy; the 1.3 was swiftly replaced by a 1.4, while a 1.6 petrol engine powered the range-topping models, including a very lively Polo GTI.

Volkswagen was able to broaden the appeal of the Polo by drawing on cars made elsewhere by the massive car company. In 1995 it added four-door saloon and five-door estate derivatives, which were actually versions of the SEAT Ibiza MkII and sourced from Spain. However, as the Ibiza was itself Polo/Golf-based, they fitted seamlessly into the line-up.

◄ Stuck on your Polo's colour? The factory-built Harlequin edition offered them all.

➤ For a supermini, the Polo's refinement was extraordinary, reflecting its Golf origins.

BMW 5 SERIES, 1995

Here we have arrived at one of the true highlights of the 1990s car canon. It was the fourth generation of 5 Series since the large sports saloon arrived in 1972, but there's little doubt that this E39 iteration represents the absolute peak of perfection of the genre. The 2.3-litre 523i and 2.8-litre 528i in particular are absolutely legendary members of BMW's most elite.

The concept was much as before, a large four-door saloon with a straight-six engine up-front feeding power to the rear wheels. The balance of these key assets was matched by the fantastic way BMW's engineers had refined the all-aluminium suspension and other driveline components to provide the most accomplished compromise between sporty handling and limousine-like ride quality. An agile and precise car to drive fast, it could also cruise serenely at any speed, and the all-new rack-and-pinion steering for the four- and six-cylinder models (the V8s used a different system) was immediately among the best in the world.

A predominantly aluminium chassis structure and a wind-cheating profile with a super-low drag factor of 0.27 just added to the towering efficiency of the car. The seats were supremely comfortable and

The svelte lines of the all-new 5 Series swathed a brilliant new executive saloon.

WHAT THEY SAID AT THE TIME

'The finest saloon car in the world just got a whole lot better. Imagine th suppleness of a Jaguar XJ8 matched to the iron stability of a Mercedes S-class and the body control of a good sports car.'

Autocar magazine in April 1996 on the £29,990 528i SE.

▲ The estate version of the 5 Series was called the Touring and was thoroughly family-friendly.

▼ A 520i, at the opposite end of the spectrum from the high-octane M5 but just as beautifully built.

support-giving and in this latest 5 Series the spacious rear seat was now a match for those up front.

Every single aspect of the car seemed to be perfectly attuned to the others, creating a sports saloon like nothing else available. In parallel, BMW was right up to date on its safety systems, with every model boasting front and side airbags – the latter including the head-protecting curtain type – seatbelt pre-tensioners, anti-lock brakes, traction control and one of the first in-built satnav systems using, at first, maps on CD.

WHO LOVED IT?

If you had the money to buy the very best, then here it was. A wide spread of engines, including diesels, catered for a lot of different drivers, a small number of whom chose the ultimate M5 performance model. We should not forget, though, the excellent Touring estate derivative, its tailgate opening window section being a signature feature. Even today, enthusiasts have a hushed reverence for the brilliant E39.

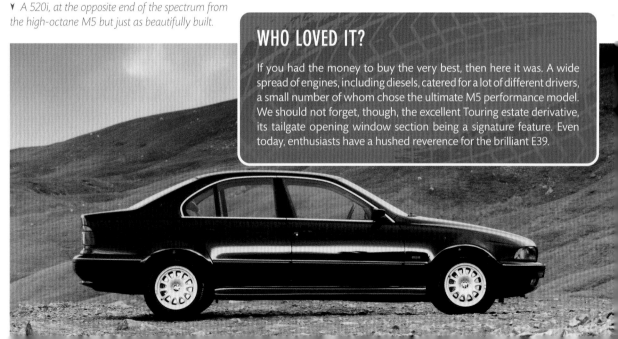

DAEWOO NEXIA & ESPERO, 1995 & MATIZ, 1998

Up to this point in this 1990s narrative, we've gone back in time to kick the tyres of many significant cars; great examples of design, performance, technological advancement, and sometimes just plain old practicality. These two, though, are memorable for different reasons. They were the first mass-produced cars of modern times to be sold directly to the public by the manufacturer itself, rather than via franchised dealers.

Daewoo was a new, tricky-to-pronounce (you were meant to say 'Day-oo') name from South Korea. For several years, the company had produced the Vauxhall Astra MkII under licence for General Motors in the USA,

which sold it across North America at rock-bottom prices as the Pontiac LeMans. Now that car had become obsolete in the West, Daewoo spruced it up as the 1.5-litre Nexia and started selling it under its own brand name. There was a choice of three, four or five doors.

↑ Nexia, please: Daewoo found plenty of Brits to buy its wares direct.

↗ The Nexia saloon seemingly offered great value, but its depreciation was epic.

WHAT THEY SAID AT THE TIME

'As expected, equipment levels are very good and include such sensible kit as power steering, anti-lock brakes and a driver's side airbag. All you have to do is put up with a car whose abilities are firmly entrenched in the '80s ... dreadful ride, soggy handling, mediocre refinement and poor interior packaging.'

Autocar magazine in August 1995 on the £8,445 Nexia 1.5 GLi.

Alongside it in Daewoo's own network of local show-rooms stood the Espero, a larger 1.8-litre four-door saloon whose Bertone-of-Italy-styled lines hid the mechanical workings of the even more ancient Vauxhall Cavalier MkII.

▲ *Not one of Daewoo's dogs; the little Matiz was a nifty three-cylinder city car.*

WHO LOVED IT?

Daewoo's direct-selling scheme and massive advertising campaign made a big splash. In 1996 it had bagged 1 per cent of the British market. People initially rushed to buy, and that included some big fleet orders from organisations like NHS Scotland. Customers, though, didn't get off lightly; values of the cars sank like stones on the second-hand market. A bizarre rebrand under the Chevrolet name did little to help. And although Mercedes-Benz has since adopted the direct-selling ethos, the rest of the industry has stuck with traditional car dealers.

The cars themselves were serviceable but mediocre in most major respects. However, the 'no-haggle' purchasing package really was innovative. The competitive prices (the Nexia started at a paltry £8,295) came with a three-year warranty, three years' free servicing and three years' AA membership, while freebies thrown in included one year's road tax, number plates, a tank of petrol and even a mobile phone.

Although Daewoo wasn't around for long in the British market, in 1988 it produced its only truly interesting machine, the attractive Matiz city car with a three-cylinder engine. The Matiz was created under the eye of former Porsche engineer (and later Aston Martin boss) Dr Ulrich Bez, and its development was handled by Daewoo's Technical Centre at Worthing, West Sussex.

◄ *They called it the Espero, but inside this bigger Daewoo was the very old-school Vauxhall Cavalier.*

FORD GALAXY & VOLKSWAGEN SHARAN, 1995

By the mid 1990s, the MPV (multi-passenger vehicle) market sector was getting too big for mainstream car-makers to ignore. It wasn't just as hotel shuttle transport, either. They were being bought by families in preference to big estate cars and featured strongly in the daily school-run chaos in towns across the country.

But while Renault and Toyota did their own thing, Ford and Volkswagen elected to share costs by jointly developing one neat design of seven-seater metal box and opening a new plant in Portugal to produce it.

Looked like a bus but drove like a car – the Ford Galaxy boosted MPV popularity.

The interior of the Volkswagen Sharan shows the many ways its seven-seater layout could be arranged.

WHO LOVED IT?

In the UK, it was the Galaxy that dominated thanks to Fo[rd's] leading position in the market, with Volkswagen sell[ing] many fewer Sharans. Cars like these sounded the de[ath] knell for the biggest estates, typified by the Ford Scor[pio] and Vauxhall Omega. Once the versatility of this big seve[n-] seater had been sampled – for business or pleasure – it w[as] hard to return to a 'normal' station wagon.

The result was the Ford Galaxy you see here, along with Volkswagen's identical Sharan, plus a version for VW-owned brand SEAT, the Alhambra. Nominally a 50:50 joint venture, Volkswagen led the project, furnishing its 1.9-litre four-cylinder turbodiesel and 2.8-litre petrol VR6 engines, while Ford provided its own four-cylinder 2-litre petrol unit. It had front-wheel drive, with Ford manual gearboxes or VW automatic transmission.

The cavernous interior used a cocktail of Ford and Volkswagen parts but the key thing was its versatile space – considerably more than the Renault Espace. The five seats at the back could be folded or removed, and the front two chairs could swivel round to face the rear. Yet despite being something of a mini-minibus, the Galaxy/Sharan was surprisingly nimble and enjoyable to drive.

Ford ducked out of the partnership in 2007, replacing the Galaxy with a new MPV developed in tandem with the S-Max. That left the Portugal factory to VW, which continued making the original Sharan and Alhambra there until 2010.

Volkswagen Sharan demonstrating how rapidly it could become essential to the family.

ROVER 200, 1995

There was still some feisty independent spirit at Rover in the early 1990s, despite its long-standing joint venture with Honda that gave the Japanese company the upper hand in creating new cars, plus a 20 per cent shareholding in what had once been British Leyland.

The Metro was knocking on and under siege from some fiercely good competitors, and bosses at the Longbridge factory in Birmingham suddenly realised they would need something else to keep the production lines rolling at capacity. Fortunately, the design department had a neat little car they'd been longing to build, all fully worked out. It arose from a chat among the youthful design team; when asked which of them would buy a new Rover themselves, almost no one put up their hands, and so they decided to create the sort of car they'd choose to own.

The compact and stylish 200 put a bit of British pride back into Rover.

WHO LOVED IT?

The 200 range helped transform an affordable Rov from being an 'old man's car' to something young buyers would seriously consider instead of a Peuge 306 (against which the 200 was, admittedly, pret cramped inside). Demand was always somewh suppressed by Rover's higher-price strategy, ar annual UK sales peaked at 64,000 in 1998.

Rover engineers used existing parts and suspension units to cut costs and make the 200 viable.

Interior of the five-door 200; there was a three-door too, neither of them especially roomy.

That's how the neat and sporty design of Project SK3 arose, with its slim chrome grille, 'bobtail' back end, 15in wheels and stylish interior. The clever part was in its use of various existing unseen parts, such as suspension from the old Austin Maestro, only retuned for sportier handling. That way, the investment needed to build it was tiny, and designers found clever ways to produce a new dashboard.

Size-wise, it was bigger than a Metro but smaller than the Honda-based Rover 400, plugging a sizeable chasm in Rover's line-up, and there was a choice of three or five doors. The engines were variants of Rover's all-aluminium K-series, from 1.4- to 1.8-litre and with the range-topping 200 Vi using the 143bhp variable-valve-timed unit direct from the MGF. There was also a 2-litre turbodiesel.

This ingeniously designed, all-British 200 played a vital role in keeping Rover going throughout the 1990s.

VAUXHALL VECTRA, 1995

Examining the life and times of Vauxhall's medium-sized offering for the latter half of the 1990s, the Vectra gets a drubbing at odds with the huge number you'd have found on Britain's roads by the turn of the Millennium. Was it as shabby as Jeremy Clarkson, and other acerbic critics, would have you believe?

True, a car like this didn't need to have such lifeless steering, ponderous handling and leaden responses. The Peugeot 405 of seven years earlier easily managed to combine comfort with sportiness and eagerness. It was the same with the Vectra driving position, unnecessarily hampered by no steering-wheel adjustment.

Then again, the Vectra was conceived chiefly for bulk fleet (rather than private) purchase and long-distance motorway driving. Hence the tall gearing for relaxed cruising, superior fuel economy and good-quality interior. Indeed, the whole car was very well constructed under that sleek, if slightly anonymous, styling. And it was built in Luton, Vauxhall's British factory, whereas the rival Mondeo was an import, so the Vectra was actively helpful to the country's economy.

The sleek integration of the door mirrors was the most interesting aspect of the Vectra's exterior ...

A wide range of engines was offered in the four-door saloon, five-door hatch and (from 1996) five-door estate. Starting with a basic four-cylinder 1.6-litre, the petrol line-up culminated in a 2.5-litre V6, with most drivers allocated a 16-valve 1.8- or 2-litre motor. The initial 1.7-litre Isuzu-made diesel engine was swiftly replaced by Vauxhall's own, punchier 2-litre in diesel and turbodiesel forms.

O LOVED IT?

range was huge, and trawling through the engine ces and trim levels was an evening's work. For one selecting their new company car, that was a sant task, and the Vectra sold strongly. For anyone ing excitement, though, this was not the one, despite khall's saloon-car racing programme and sportily ned SRi and limited-edition derivatives.

↗ *Five-door models made up the bulk of Vectra sales, aimed at motorway-bashing corporate employees.*

↘ *Jeremy Clarkson may have been stony-faced but the Vectra estate was an ideal load-lugger for many.*

In March 1999, a revamp sharpened up everything from the handling to the detail styling, although it barely lifted the Vectra's reputation for functional ordinariness.

AUDI A3 & S3, 1996

Audi was on to a winner from the off with its brilliant A3, this being the five-door version added in 1999.

Audi provided an enormous boost to its appeal with the A3. While BMW already offered its 3 Series Compact as a three-door hatchback with an unquestionably premium badge, this front-wheel-drive Audi was even more in tune with a generation accustomed to driving Volkswagen Golfs. Tasteful restraint, a brilliant drive, and superb quality were all combined in one very neat car.

A line-up of 1.6- and 1.8-litre petrol and 1.9-litre turbo-diesel four-cylinder engines covered all bases for the size of car. Typical of what many buyers chose once first UK deliveries of the A3 began in December 1996 was the five-valves-per-cylinder 1.8-litre with 148bhp on tap, making this A3 a potent 135mph car.

Audi struggled for the first three years of the A3's life to keep pace with demand. And then, in 1999, it expanded the appeal of the car in several different directions. Increased practicality was tackled with a five-door body option, while performance in a wintry context was catered for with the 1.8T Quattro with up to 178bhp and four-wheel drive for icy alpine roads. There was a different four-wheel drive system for the overtly sporting S3 of 1999, cutting in when needed as the driver enjoyed flinging around this 207bhp hot hatch with its wide alloy wheels and body-hugging Recaro leather seats.

The neat and purposeful, if a little gloomy, interior of the Audi A3 Sport.

WHAT THEY SAID AT THE TIME

'If you are in the market for a safe, classy and enjoyable hatchback there simply is no better car. Audi has arrived. It is, quite simply, the best car in its class, bar none. The A3 also handles better than any other front-drive Audi to date.'

Autocar magazine in September 1996 on the £17,591 A3 1.8 Sport

↖ *Audi's slick A3 design hid a chassis that would be used to underpin numerous other VW group models.*

➤ *Pumped-up Audi S3 Quattro with 225bhp and four-wheel drive.*

WHO LOVED IT?

Audi had possibly its biggest ever hit on its hands with the first A3. This one more than any other helped to widen the reach for VW's profitable upmarket car brand. The package was perfectly sized and formed, and the first A3 remained in huge demand both new and second-hand until a new model arrived in 2002.

Contemporary critics sang the praises of the A3's detailed aspects, such as the ease with which almost anyone could find the perfect driving position within the roomy and beautifully finished cabin. They also loved the way the car handled. This was crucial praise indeed because the all-new platform introduced with the A3 soon found its way into numerous Volkswagen group products, including the all-important next-generation Golf itself.

FORD KA, 1996 & PUMA, 1997

London's Royal College of Art was very proud of the Ford Ka, which is supposed to be pronounced like 'car' even though company insiders are also known to say 'cah', as in 'cat'. Its startlingly original lines were originally penned at the South Kensington design school in 1992 by one of its students, Chris Svensson of Sunderland, and were brought to life by a newly adventurous Ford when he worked there, as part of the firm's 'New Edge' styling movement.

Inside and out, curved lines intersected everywhere for a new take on the city car, with bold lobe shapes for the dashboard, hatchback and seats, while prominent, moulded plastic nose, tail and wheel-arch sections were perfect for warding off parking knocks on crowded streets.

Quite apart from the leap in design imagination, it didn't cost Ford much to put the Ka on sale. It was based on the Fiesta floorpan with basic and long-serving 1.3-litre Endura-E overhead-valve engines that, in various forms, had been around since the 1950s. The cute little Ka was still lively, though – cheap to run and very reliable. It was also great fun to drive, with nimble handling and good road adhesion in tight corners. Hardly fast but always entertaining, and you could order niceties like power steering, alloy wheels and air-con.

WHAT THEY SAID AT THE TIME

'We found the Ka and its modest horsepower a real hoot over moorland roads. It has no bad habits. The slowest car of the year, and one of our absolute favourites.'

Autocar magazine in October 1995 on the £8,195 Ka 2.

'Three things stand out on the Puma and enable it to dominate the compact coupé market: its styling, its chassis, and the fact that it is simply a cracking good car to drive.'

Autocar magazine in March 1998 on the £14,725 Puma 1.7i.

The radical looks of the Ka kicked off Ford's so-called 'New Edge' design movement.

Ford was getting adept at generating niche models spun off from the Fiesta. In 1997, it followed up the Ka with the slinky little Puma, a two-door coupé that was a distinct cut above the rival Vauxhall Tigra for low-cost exhilaration. The peppy Zetec-SE engines in 1.4-, 1.6- and 1.7-litre sizes gave zip to the sparkling chassis. Even if you missed out on owning one of these super little machines, you may recall the TV advertising campaign that cleverly lifted clips of Steve McQueen from the film *Bullitt*.

▶ *Scratch-proof plastic wheel arches, nose and tail sections made the Ka very city-proof.*

◀ *A huge order from BT gave rise to the UK-only Ka van, later offered to other buyers too.*

▼ *The delightful Ford Puma was, just like the Ka, based on the mainstream Fiesta.*

HO LOVED THEM?

e Ka was a hit, with 490,000 sold right up until
08, and led the British city-car market for years.
even bought a large batch kitted out as tiny vans
its engineers to nip around in. Likewise, the Puma,
ough sold exclusively in Europe for just four years,
oved very popular, with 133,000 finding buyers.

1990s
SPORTS CARS

A striking trend of this decade that rarely gains much recognition was the return of the traditional two-seater sports car. The standard-bearer for this welcome revival was undoubtedly the Mazda MX-5 (see p.10), a car born of Japan's bewilderment at Britain having thrown away its leadership in this sector by axing its MG Midget, MGB, Triumph Spitfire and Triumph TR7 by the early 1980s, and not bothering to replace any of them. Likewise, the MX-5 recreated the sparkling driving pleasure of the Lotus Elan, another of Britain's classics long consigned to history.

▲ *A Honda CRX from 1997, on which a roof panel could be ordered that slid electrically into the boot to open the car up.*

➤ *The 1990s played host to the second generation of Toyota's mid-engined MR2, which could be had with this breezy T-bar roof option.*

▼ *The 1992 Reliant Sabre was a short-lived attempt by the British three-wheeler maker to carve out a spot for itself in the sports-car market.*

TVR's beautiful Griffith was in fact a fearsome performer with its Rover V8 powerplant.

The market for two-seaters with wind-in-the-hair exhilaration had been largely sustained by demand from America's 'sunshine states', California in particular, but the reason the cars died out was a US law of the late 1970s that never actually came to pass. Manufacturers were spooked into believing that North American legislation would outlaw convertible cars on the grounds of occupant safety in the event that the car flipped over in a crash. It led to the soft-top Mustang, Corvette and Cadillac Eldorado all dying out by 1976, with other manufacturers quietly dropping any more ragtop vehicles from their future plans.

The Chimaera turned out to be TVR's all-time bestseller, and many owners found it an easy, comfortable and very fast roadster to live with day to day.

Blast from the past: the venerable MGB returned in its new R-V8 guise as MG sports cars came back on sale in 1992.

▾ *This very rare beast is the Caterham 21 of 1994; although unsuccessful, the British government was keen to encourage newcomers to enter the market by easing the car-building rules for low volumes.*

Despite the industry's worst fears, the ban was never actually enacted. And so the US market eagerly lapped up the new Mazda from 1989. Other Japanese two-seaters already offered some fresh air; the second-generation, mid-engined 1989 Toyota MR2 had lift-out roof panels and the dinky little 1992 Honda Civic CRX had a steel top that could be slid electronically into the boot to let the sun in. But neither offered the carefree roadster character of the MX-5.

The all-new MGF of 1995 was unusual in being a mid-engined open two-seater; it received a warm reception from enthusiasts.

There were some small signs of life to indicate that the British sports car wasn't completely dead. Reliant had its plastic-bodied Scimitar SST on the market in 1990, with a choice of mild Ford 1.4 or vivid Nissan 1.8 turbo engines, joining the mid-engined Ginetta G32 and front-engined Ginetta G33 as part of the diverse specialist car scene in this country. Then, in 1992, Blackpool's TVR released its Rover V8-engined Griffith and Chimeara sports cars, the former a ferocious, out-and-out high-performance car and the latter a more civilised and practical machine for daily driving and the one that became the marque's all-time bestseller.

▲ With its four tiny headlights and startling Pininfarina lines, Alfa Romeo's new 1995 Spider offered mould-breaking Italian styling, and some superb engines turning the front wheels.

▼ Technical secrets of the MGF exposed, including the interconnected Hydragas suspension system and the K-series engine.

Indeed, the government was keen to foster new car-making enterprise when, in 1993, Low-Volume Type Approval was introduced – a set of rules that allowed small manufacturers of interesting cars to survive and/or flourish. It permitted them to make a limited number of specialist cars without the crippling burden of full new car design mandates, and companies like Caterham, with its new 21 model; Marcos; and Westfield all embraced the move to become more credible as proper carmakers.

▲ *Live Aid organiser and rock star Bob Geldof trying hard not to look proud of his brand new Alfa Romeo Spider V6 3.0 24v.*

▼ *BMW's Z3 roadster was new for 1996 and shared its chassis with the 3 Series.*

*The all-metal roof of the supercharged 1996 Mercedes-Benz
SLK folded away into the boot to create an open two-seater.*

As all of this was happening, there were moves to put MG back into the sports-car mainstream. The famous octagonal logo had appeared on souped-up versions of Austins throughout the 1980s, but now the renamed Rover Group took the audacious decision to reintroduce the MGB. In 1992 the old warhorse reappeared as the MG R-V8, sporting a muscular new makeover to the familiar shape, and a 3.9-litre Rover V8 engine under the bonnet. A limited edition of 2,000 was planned, and they all sold out immediately. But this was really a preview of an all-new MG that would take its bow in 1995. The MGF was radical for the marque in that it offered a mid-mounted K-Series engine in a unique two-seater body, with a novel interconnected Hydragas suspension system adapted from the one featured in the Rover Metro.

➤ Porsche eschewed its traditional rear engine for a mid-mounted one in its highly desirable 1996 Boxster.

▼ This cute Suzuki Cappuccino could give you a real lift with its tiny turbocharged motor and rear-wheel drive.

The Elise of 1996 was the full-on sports car Lotus fans ha[ve] been begging for for years, a paragon of great handling [&] ingenious construction.

The MGF, which proved extremely popular, was the first serious challenge to the MX-5 in the new car market. But it was by no means the last. From Italy came two new alternatives, the 1994 Fiat Barchetta (see p.72) and the all-new Alfa Romeo Spider a year later, both front-wheel drive cars with very contrasting styles but bags of character.

And next came no less than three sports-car challengers from Germany: the BMW Z3 in 1995 and the Porsche Boxster and Mercedes-Benz SLK in 1996. Although all considerably costlier than the Mazdas and MGs that were a fairly common sight on British roads – occasionally, when the rain held off, even with their roofs down – they were all radical in their different ways. The BMW was based on the 3 Series and built in the USA, and it managed to land a starring role in the James Bond film *Goldeneye*, with Pierce Brosnan. The Boxster featured a 2.7-litre flat-six engine with water-cooling, in place of the air-cooled motor in the evergreen 911, which was mid- rather than rear-mounted. Meanwhile, the compact Mercedes offered a super-charged four-cylinder engine and a metal coupé roof that could be electronically folded away into the boot.

In Japan there was an unusual take on the ultra-small two-seater roadster with the 1991 Suzuki Cappuccino. This cute little car was designed within the parameters of the country's *kei* car rules so it could enjoy lower taxation costs and qualify for a parking space in crowded cities. This meant it weighed just 725kg (1,598lb) and was powered by a three-cylinder, double overhead-camshaft 657cc engine, with a correspondingly tiny turbocharger to give it some extra kick. As it had a front-mounted engine with rear-wheel drive, ideal near-50:50 weight distribution made it quite accomplished in handling, and the two occupants could either have the roof fixed in place, the overhead panel removed, or a completely open car with the glass rear screen lowered out of sight.

But this was probably not the sort of car to appeal to the racing driver lurking inside every keen motorist. For a sports car offering the ultimate in no-compromise handling the obvious choice was the diminutive Lotus Elise, launched to multiple plaudits in 1995. With its bonded-aluminium inner structure, glass-fibre panels and aluminium Rover engine behind the shallow two-seater cockpit, it was a sports car based on the first principles of total driver immersion in the art of roadholding at high speeds. There weren't even any carpets in this street racer, and there was little to touch it ... apart, perhaps, from the similarly 'raw' 1996 Renault Sport Spider, where the first examples of this mid-engined go-kart didn't even feature a windscreen ...

Are those flies in his teeth? Could be, because the Renault Sport Spider didn't, initially, come with a windscreen.

RENAULT MEGANE SCÉNIC, 1996

This high-riding family five-seater was by far the most noteworthy car in the brand-new Megane range, which arrived in 1996 to take the mid-range baton from the somewhat forgettable Renault 19.

▲ *Plenty to smile about in the highly kid-friendly interior of the Scénic.*

◄ *Renault underestimated demand for its mould-breaking Scénic by a factor of five.*

WHAT THEY SAID AT THE TIME

'The car that started the trend for mini-MPVs, it's still hugely appealing. But the new Vauxhall Zafira drives better – and it offers seven seats. There are new features like a facia-mounted coolbox ... this is for the benefit of the kids.'

Autocar magazine in September 1999 on the £17,500 Scénic 2.0 16v.

There had been a compact MPV long before, in the rectilinear shape of the 1983 Nissan Prairie. But with the Scénic – with front-wheel drive and a panoply of four-cylinder petrol and diesel engines from 1.4- to 2-litre – came an entirely new take on interior space adaptable to the needs and wants of any young family. It was created specially for the kids. The three seats in the back could slide backwards and forwards, with a reclining mechanism for naps and tables in the front seat backs for colouring-in or making things. Alternatively, the centre seat could be folded flat so an optional toybox or cool-box could be clipped in; or a seat could be removed and the two remaining ones repositioned to give more elbow room for teenagers, who might have plugged their Walkmans (remember, this was way before even the iPod existed ...) into the standard power socket so they couldn't hear Mum and Dad droning on upfront. The Scénic offered a warren of hidden trays, luggage cupboards, underfloor cellars and secret compartments, while the parcel shelf was the world's first with three different height settings.

The whole interior concept was overseen by British designer Anthony Grade, younger brother of TV tycoon Michael. He made sure the rear seats all had a great view out of the front of the car, just like the bigger seven-seater Espace. 'Once you give buyers a product with the space, you can then leave it up to them what they do with it,' he said. Rivals, though, followed thick and fast, and the car entered the 2000s facing stiff competition from the Citroën Picasso, Fiat Multipla and Vauxhall Zafira.

WHO LOVED IT?

Initially marketed as the world's first 'Multi-Activity Car', the Scénic set the template for many other compact MPVs to follow, including the Citroën Xsara Picasso, Vauxhall Zafira and Volkswagen Touran. The Scénic was phenomenally successful from the start, taking Renault utterly by surprise. It was soon making 2,500 examples a day, five times the original forecast, and in just a year accounted for 35 per cent of all Megane orders. It was crowned 1997 European Car Of The Year.

Deft touches abounded inside the car, such as this pull-out, under-seat storage drawer.

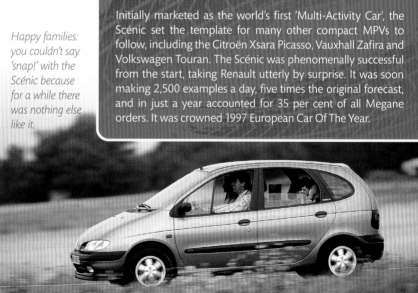

Happy families: you couldn't say 'snap!' with the Scénic because for a while there was nothing else like it.

ŠKODA OCTAVIA, 1996

The Octavia was a remarkable car, not just for its excellent size-to-value ratio – in Ford terms, you got a Mondeo for the price of an Escort – but also for the competence of the five-door hatchback itself. At the cheaper end of the market, people had been buying Protons, Hyundais and Daewoos and putting up with second-raters. The Octavia changed all that in an instant.

Revealed just before Christmas in 1996, the Octavia shared its structural fundamentals with the Audi A3 (and several subsequent VW Group cars), and likewise made use of the company's comprehensive roster of four-cylinder petrol and diesel engines, from a meek 1.4-litre petrol to a quite feisty 1.8-litre turbodiesel, with familiar manual and automatic transmissions. They were all built in Škoda's Czech factory, though, and the chunky exterior design was unique to the marque; a capacious estate was added in 1998.

It seemed incredible that this budget-priced car was almost as big as a Volkswagen Passat, with an absolutely gigantic boot. From the quality and support of the seats to the composed and comfortable road manners, people searched in vain for something to moan about, but of the old Škoda design and quality drawbacks of the 1980s there was no sign.

No one had really considered Škodas as performance cars before, but the Octavia changed that too. The 150bhp vRS model, with its turbocharged 1.8-litre engine, was a 146mph slingshot that could sprint to 60mph from rest in under 8sec. Škoda took them racing and rallying, and little wonder the vRS became a firm favourite with budget-conscious British police forces as an effective, and unmarked, pursuit 'Q-car'.

Škoda's 146mph vRS was a favourite with British police forces as a stealthy pursuit car.

WHAT THEY SAID AT THE TIME

'VW's faith in Škoda has been well rewarded. This is budget family car motoring at its very best. Driveability is a major draw but economy is outstanding. On test it averaged 42.7mpg.'

Autocar magazine in July 1998 on the £14,199 Octavia 1.9TDI GLX.

➤ *Here's the very trusty Octavia estate, a favourite in the UK as a hardworking minicab.*

⌄ *See it for dust; Škoda took the Octavia rallying to prove its worth and raise its profile.*

WHO LOVED IT?

Minicab drivers – Britain's private-hire fleets were soon packed with Octavias, running people to and from stations all over the country and taking drunken partygoers home in the wee small hours of the weekend. It was cheap to buy or lease, roomy and robust, and easy to maintain. Canny private buyers mopped up the rest.

ALFA ROMEO 156, 1997

Back on form: that was the verdict on Alfa's compact sports saloon revealed in autumn 1997 and sitting temptingly in British showrooms just after Christmas. In stark contrast to some of the strangely unattractive smaller Alfas of the late 1980s and early 1990s, the design team had revisited the curvaceous classics littering its 1950s and '60s heritage for the 156. Its shapely, purposeful body featured a dramatic, shield-shaped grille, undulating flanks and nose and tail shaped to almost eradicate cumbersome-looking bumpers, while the interior – especially with body-hugging seats upholstered in rich, yellow Italian leather – was pretty close to gorgeous.

Can you handle it? Rear-door release was cunningly concealed to maintain the 156's sporting good looks.

The shield-shaped Alfa grille and offset front number plate oozed Italian character.

There was Italian passion under the bonnet too, with a choice of sparkling 1.6-, 1.8- and 2-litre Twin-Spark four-cylinder engines, a four-cylinder 1.9 or five-cylinder 2.4 turbodiesel and – at the pinnacle of the range – Alfa Romeo's fantastic 2.5-litre V6 with one of the most exciting soundtracks of any engine in an attainable mainstream car. They all drove through the front wheels, and while there was a four-wheel drive option in Europe, it was withheld from the UK.

WHO LOVED IT?

No genuine Alfa fan could fail to be proud of the 156, and the cocktail of alluring looks and scintillating performance was potent enough to bring plenty of new buyers into the fold. The Italian police force bought loads of them. They could misbehave a little as second-hand cars but, hey, that's part of the Italian character too ...

This was one Alfa you'd love to own, and it saw something of a renaissance for the hallowed Italian marque. There were so many lovely details you could show your friends, such as the hidden external handles for the rear doors carefully designed to blend in with the window frame and make the car look like a GT coupé. Popping the bonnet to see that beautiful V6 motor was an experience in itself. But the true appeal was on the road, where the sleek Alfa saloon – and, from 2000, an equally attractive Sportwagon estate – was everything you could hope for in terms of sporty enjoyment.

LAND ROVER FREELANDER, 1997

Land Rover made its dramatic, if belated, step into the compact off-roader arena in 1997. The market for small, family-friendly 4x4s had exploded ever since the introduction of the Toyota RAV4, and now here was a startling new British contender, which had actually been on various drawing boards since the late 1980s.

In fact, the most surprising facet was under the Freelander's bulging lines, because this was the first Land Rover ever to do away entirely with a separate chassis frame. The big wheels and high ground clearance carried a welded monocoque body/chassis unit, which could be had as a five-door station wagon or a two-door semi-convertible called a Softback, which could also be ordered with a hardtop to seal it for winter. Engines were from Rover's K-series petrol and L-series diesel families.

The clanking mechanism of a two-speed transfer box was replaced by a front-mounted Intermediate Reduction Drive and a viscous coupling unit in the driveshaft to the rear axle for permanent four-wheel drive; downhill control to co-ordinate front and back wheels came from an electronic 'Hill Descent Control' system employing the foundation ABS braking system to regulate the Freelander's speed. There were no low-range ratios or any locking differential, but then Freelanders were never going to be used by the SAS – there was still excellent off-road traction in line with the Freelander's leisure aspirations.

Novel: the all-new Freelander came as convertible 'Softback' or five-door 'Hardback'.

▲ *A Hill Descent Control co-ordinated the Freelander's four-wheel drive system for off-road antics.*

▼ *Turning a page: inside the Softback edition of the Freelander, soon a pan-European success.*

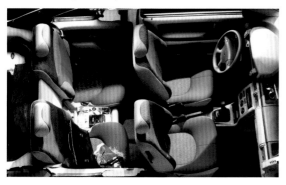

WHO LOVED IT?

Pretty much instantly, the Freelander became the bestseller in its class, not just in the UK but across the whole of mainland Europe. What it proved was that car buyers were drawn to a commanding driving position, the security of four-wheel drive for on- and occasional off-road driving, a rugged stance and a versatile interior. The raw capability to cut through jungle just wasn't needed.

Strangely, although Rover and Honda had pooled development of other cars, the Japanese company chose to create its own rival in parallel to the Freelander, the CR-V. For Honda, though, the inclination to stay independent was vindicated when BMW bought Rover Group from British Aerospace and the offended Japanese firm immediately severed all links with its longstanding partner. Going on sale just before the Freelander, Honda's five-door sport utility vehicle was built in Britain too, at Honda's own Swindon plant. It established an excellent name for itself for faultless quality and reliability.

WHAT THEY SAID AT THE TIME

'The 119bhp 1.8-litre engine is smooth and responsive. It has all of what is good about Land Rovers. It isn't as swift as the indecently quick RAV4, but it has more grip in corners, and excellent body control.'

Autocar magazine in February 1998 on the £15,570 Freelander 1.8 Softback.

MERCEDES-BENZ A-CLASS, 1997

Here is the controversial small Mercedes that took aim at the VW Golf but was thrown off course by an elk.

WHAT THEY SAID AT THE TIME

'The steering is lifeless and easily corrupted by engine torque, while the ride quality lacks the supple approach of its rivals. The new 1.6-litre engine, on the other hand, is a triumph, combining refinement, performance and economy. It remains a flawed diamond.'

Autocar magazine in June 1998 on the £15,490 A160.

The German company was determined to expand the scope of its range outwards from large luxury cars, and decided that the A-Class would be its first front-wheel drive offering, with a transversely mounted engine. To keep it compact – and it really was tiny, even shorter than the diminutive Ford Ka despite being a tall, five-door hatchback – the four-cylinder power units were mounted very low down, almost under the floor.

Hitting the skids; Mercedes rectified the A-Class's early tendency to tumble.

WHO LOVED IT

Despite its faltering start, the A-Class ended up selling 1.1m examples until the second-generation model arrived in 2004, a fair few of which came to the UK. However, it then developed a rogue reputation for reliability, which made it a risky car to buy second-hand (it was quite expensive new). For Mercedes, trying to manufacture cars more cheaply, the A-Class experience was a bruising one.

The A-Class was a bold move for Mercedes-Benz as it took on the VW Golf and its ilk.

The company was anxious to safeguard the venerable marque's hard-won reputation for safety innovation, and so designed the A-Class platform 'sandwich' so that, in the event of a severe front-end shunt, the engine and transmission would be pushed under the car, rather than intrude into the cabin and injure the occupants' legs.

Unfortunately, all this clever thinking was undermined by a Swedish motoring magazine. It subjected an early A-Class to its routine high-speed, wintry, obstacle-avoidance manoeuvre, nicknamed the 'elk test', and the A-Class promptly flipped over after its sudden swerve.

It was all very embarrassing for Mercedes, although it was admirably thorough in its quick response. The 2,500 cars sold so far were all recalled and it spent a frenzied three months modifying the suspension and designing a stability control system. When the car was relaunched its handling vice had been fixed. In 2001, the company also offered a long-wheelbase model with a stretch of 5.7in to provide more rear passenger space. Overall, the car scored highly for its interior and fuel economy, less well for driving pleasure.

Inner secrets of the A-Class included a 'sandwich' construction to push the engine underneath in a serious shunt.

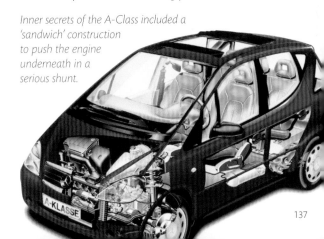

AUDI TT, 1998

In the final year-and-a-half of the decade you might just have seen the first few examples of this exciting new two-seater Audi on British roads. It was easy to spot because it looked like absolutely nothing else around, with its smooth, tight contours and super-low roofline. Audi's design team had consulted the history books for inspiration, which came not just from the aerodynamic Auto Union speed-record cars of the 1930s but also the sleek Bauhaus design movement of the same era. The TT title also celebrated the past, in this case the victories scored by German NSU motorcycles in the Tourist Trophy races.

The TT – this is the 3.2 Quattro – looked unlike anything else on the road.

WHO LOVED IT?

The TT, in either open or closed form, was one of the most distinctive sports cars on the road. Definitely one for dating couples or newlyweds, as the rear seats in the coupé were torture even for children. It helped transform Audis from sensible vehicles to objects of desire ...

⋏ *Two-seater Roadster version of the TT combined fresh air and thrills.*

⋎ *Early TTs could be hairy at very high speeds, so Audi added a discreet tail spoiler for extra downforce.*

The retro-futuristic fastback styling outside and the snug, aluminium-accented interior was even more remarkable when you discovered that, underneath, the platform was shared with the VW Golf and even the Škoda Octavia. Still, the whole driveline was tuned for performance driving, in league with the 145mph top speed and acceleration from 0 to 60mph in a mere 6.1sec. The standard turbocharged 1.8-litre engine offered 180bhp but there was also a 225bhp version, in addition to a spyder convertible and a Quattro four-wheel drive option.

The Audi was a potent and responsive machine – indeed, a little too responsive. All the cars delivered in the UK at the tail end of 1998 were recalled. The TT had proved to be worryingly skittish when changing direction at very high speeds, and the company quickly fixed the problem by fitting an electronic stability control system, modified suspension and a discreet tail aerofoil for added downforce to keep the TT anchored firmly to the tarmac at all times. Once sorted, Audi also offered a 250bhp 3.2-litre VR6 model, with four-wheel drive only.

FORD FOCUS MKI, 1998

Ford's replacement for the Escort shot straight to the top of its class for its sporty road manners, near-luxury-car levels of refinement, technical innovation and its sharp 'New Edge' design. Even the mighty Golf was put in the shade for all-round excellence. And most of the attributes that helped it to win the coveted European Car of the Year trophy for 1999 were finessed in the UK, at Ford's Dunton Technical Centre in Essex, although all Focus models for Europe were produced at Saarlouis in Germany.

Bridge to the future: the new Focus dispelled memories of the outgoing, inglorious Escort.

WHAT THEY SAID AT THE TIME

'On 100 arduous laps of the wretched M25, we tested the stereo, seats, glovebox and windscreen just as hard as we had previously examined the chassis, brakes and body control, and still we could find not a single significant weakness. The best car we road-tested all year.'

Autocar magazine in October 1998 on the £13,350 Focus 1.8 Zetec five-door.

Available as a three- or five-door hatchback, and shortly afterwards also as a four-door saloon and a five-door estate, the Focus gained its excellent body control and sharp steering responses – the marks of a car that could be driven spiritedly – from a brilliant driveline, including a novel multi-link rear suspension system called Control Blade. It meant that a Focus was faster and safer round corners even than top-of-the-tree sports saloons, yet the compact suspension design meant all models were still very roomy inside. In addition, it was also a safe car, with excellent brakes, high-mounted rear light clusters for top visibility, and a very good (better than the Golf MkIV) showing in independent crash test results.

Unusually, it took Ford quite a while to add a high-performance model to the line-up, with the feisty 212bhp Focus RS not arriving until 2002. It joined a range offering an already wide choice of four-cylinder engines, with petrol units from 1.4- to 2-litre and a 1.8-litre turbodiesel.

Overall, it was a car that offered superlative road manners, stylish design and keen prices. This Focus was a runaway success in the UK and right across Europe, and it would last until 2005 when the chunkier-looking MkII took on its mantle of mass-market champion.

➤ *The new Focus was an instant class leader upon launch, its exceptional dynamics impressing everyone.*

◄ *If you're going to learn to drive then it might as well be in an excellent car, like the first Focus.*

⋎ *Enthusiasts had to wait until 2002 for this turbocharged, 212bhp Focus RS, offered only in blue.*

O LOVED IT?

ou had no interest in driving other than as a means et from home to work and back, the Focus was t, comfortable, spacious and economical. But if you lled in the exhilaration of superb roadholding and ise cornering then even a low-powered Focus could e alive in your hands. These factors plus the Ford keting machine gave the Focus huge appeal.

JAGUAR S-TYPE, 1998

Jags of the 1990s had all been large, powerful cars, but the all-new S-type that lit up the 1998 London Motor Show was a confident move on the medium-sized executive/sports saloon exemplified by BMW's superb 5 Series. It was the car that the Coventry company had long yearned to produce, and with the backing of its owner Ford this was finally possible.

The new S-type styling was meant to evoke Jaguar's 1960s heyday, but it proved controversial.

The new, smaller, more affordable Jaguar would have to enjoy some economies of scale, of course, and Ford insisted Jaguar must share a basic structure with other vehicles the company made. In this case, that meant the DEW98 rolling platform with rear-wheel drive, underpinning the Lincoln LS and revived Ford Thunderbird, with independent double-wishbone suspension all round.

Apart from that, though, the S-type was Jaguar through and through, a highly self-consciously retro-looking saloon – styled by long-term Jaguar designer Geoff Lawson – evoking its 1960s namesake with an upright grille, four bulging headlights and a gracefully tapered tail. The lustrous walnut dashboard and rich leather upholstery produced an interior aura quite unlike any class competitor although, just as for the exterior, not everyone liked the cabin styling.

WHAT THEY SAID AT THE TIME

'Jaguar has produced one of the ultimate cars of the class. It didn' quite beat the seminal BMW 5 Series but it was a close-run thing. emits a delicious blend of noises on full throttle yet remains almos silent under a light load.'

Autocar magazine in March 1999 on the £37,600 S-type 4.0 V8.

◄ *S-type interior was cosseting and well-built, but once again not everyone liked the pastiche retro look.*

⋏ *The thunderous S-type R would have been a 191mph car but for a 155mph limiter!*

Starting at £27,613, it was vastly more affordable than even the cheapest XJ and would eventually be offered with 2.5- and 3-litre versions of Jaguar's new AJ-V6 alongside 4.0- and 4.2-litre AJ-V8s, plus a 4.2 super-charged S-type R whose massive 400bhp rocketed the car from 0 to 60mph in 5.3sec. This car, limited to 155mph but said to be capable without restrictor of 191mph, was Jaguar's first boy-racer machine.

WHO LOVED IT?

The S-type's nostalgia-tinged styling proved to be a splitter of opinion; even some Jag traditionalists were turned off by it. Of the car itself in everyday use, though, it offered speed, comfort and luxury, and plenty of choice, which even extended to a 2.7-litre twin-turbo V6 diesel, another Jaguar groundbreaker.

PEUGEOT 206, 1998

Peugeot has made some extraordinarily popular cars. Yet no one single model has sold as many as the 206. By 2012, 8.3m examples had been sold and, as it is still being produced in Iran, it's highly likely that, as you read this, the enormous tally will have swelled to pass the 10m mark.

Massive sales lay in store globally for the 206; this three-door car is an Entice special edition.

The 206 was the belated successor to the legendary 205 – belated in that the original plan had been not to replace the 205 at all. The French company had originally calculated that former 205 drivers could pick either the smaller 106 or the larger 306, but without a traditional, mainstream 'supermini' the marque was at a big disadvantage, and so the company's engineers created an all-new platform for the 206 that could offer a galaxy of engines from meek 1-litre petrol to hearty 1.9-litre diesel. In 1999, a 2-litre 206 GTI arrived that could attain 130mph, which was upped to 137mph for the tuned GTI 180 of 2003. In the world of hot hatches, this was something of a high-performance gem, especially as the handling of all 206s was excellent. Power-assisted steering was standard across the board.

The Peugeot 206 GTi 180 could nudge 137mph and was a favourite junior hot hatchback.

WHO LOVED IT?

The 206 was a big seller here in the UK, and the car was assembled at the company's Coventry plant to make sure that the strong demand could be met. The appealing Pininfarina-shaped design, the comfortable interior, and the frugal thirst of the mainstream 1.4- and 1.6-litre petrol versions kept Peugeot showrooms thronged with buyers.

By September 2001, half a million 206s had been built in Britain, in Coventry to be precise.

Once into the new Millennium, Peugeot added a natty 206CC model with an electrically folding metal roof, plus a five-door estate, to the three- and five-door hatchback models. There was also a tiny 206 van that was, surely, the most enjoyable-to-drive small commercial vehicle of its time. It was, perhaps, not quite the acme of Peugeot's prowess, but the French company's ability to manufacture the 206 all over the world, from South America to Malaysia and China, and tune it to local tastes that has made it an automotive phenomenon.

ROVER 75, 1998

The 75 saw Rover back on fine form, thanks to BMW's heavy investment in an all-new front-wheel drive platform that aimed to be the best in the world for refinement and road manners.

Given a clean sheet of paper, Rover's designers could finally create the luxury executive car they felt befitted this grand old name of British motoring. The subtly stylish 75 was certainly a handsome looker inside and out, its seats richly leather-upholstered, its wood trim the real thing, and its cream instruments with orange lighting a centrepiece in a very distinctive dashboard.

There were three power units; Rover's K-series in 1.8-litre straight-four and 2.5-litre V6 form, along with BMW's own turbodiesel, and transmissions were a Getrag manual or JATCO automatic, both with five speeds.

So all the elements were there, and the 75 should by rights have been one of the absolute sensations of the 1998 British Motor Show in Birmingham. Unfortunately, rifts between the management of Rover and BMW were revealed on the very day the car was announced, with dire warnings from Germany that what they called 'the English patient' had to work a whole lot harder to be viable. All of which rather overshadowed the 75's launch. But you only had to read the road test reports

Rover seemed to be back on top with its 75, a combination of tradition with modernity.

WHAT THEY SAID AT THE TIME

'The 75 has been tuned for comfort with a ride quality that is truly outstanding. As are the levels of refinement. This car is built for cruising, especially when coupled with the excellent 2497cc V6. A fine car that looks set to ensure the survival of the Rover brand.'

Autocar magazine in February 1999 on the £24,025 75 2.5 V6.

of the new car to realise it was an extremely good one. Its stiff bodyshell and sophisticated BMW-derived suspension meant it felt surprisingly sporty under a little pressure, despite its relatively soft suspension settings.

The 75's sumptuous interior included unusual cream-faced instruments.

⋏ *Smooth and serene V6 version of Rover's K-series engine tucked inside the 75's engine bay.*

⋎ *The Rover 75's layout was, in fact, the first front-wheel drive car ever to be engineered by BMW.*

WHO LOVED IT?

The pent-up desire for the return of an all-British Rover mixing the latest tech with grown-up style was right there to be exploited. Sales were initially strong. Tragically, after less than two years on sale, BMW made the abrupt decision to bail out of Rover, and the superb 75 went into the slow decline that eventually saw Rover go bust in 2005. A crying shame, that.

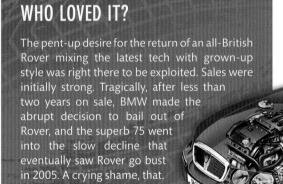

INTO THE NEW MILLENNIUM

The twilight years of the twentieth century made everyone ponder on the future as the vast unknown of the next thousand years lay just ahead. As the minutes ticked away towards midnight on 31 December 1999 and the moonlight bounced off the white plastic fabric roof of the Millennium Dome on London's time-sensitive Greenwich Peninsula, many of us were caught up in an online hysteria that was a foretaste of the social media storms that were a decade away; would all our computers go into meltdown as the so-called Millennium Bug bit, plunging an increasingly digitised world into mayhem? Everything turned out fine, and even the customary New Year's Day hangovers were reassuringly normal.

The petrol-electric hybrid Toyota Prius proved one of the most influential cars of the new century, although the first version was certainly no looker.

➤ An early Smart City-Coupé pictured in London at a time when the best way to get around the city was probably on the Routemaster buses still on faithful service in 1999/2000.

Volkswagen's New Beetle caused a massive stir, but whether its reinterpretation of the original shape – with engine shifted to the front – gelled or not is still debated even now.

The Chrysler PT Cruiser brought a bit of boldness to the family car market as its hot-rod look plundered American nostalgia.

▲ *The Audi A2 used the twin sciences of aerodynamics and lightweight, all-aluminium construction to achieve very low fuel consumption figures, but it was quite expensive.*

◄ *The first-generation Toyota Yaris quickly established itself as a small car with a lot going for it, and a wacky hologram instrument display.*

Out on the streets, though, there were some radical stirrings in the car world. The industry had seemed to reach a competitive uniformity through most of the 1990s, with the various large manufacturers competing head-to-head across most sectors with mostly very similar counterparts. But a cluster of 'disruptors' had either arrived or were on their way to shake things up.

The unusual new car with undoubtedly the most long-term significance had been unveiled in 1998 and it finally arrived in the UK in 2000. The Toyota Prius four-door saloon was the world's first production petrol-electric hybrid car. Its clever combination of electric propulsion for low-speed urban driving, energy recovery from braking to recharge the batteries, and a petrol power unit for sustained highway driving introduced the first passenger car with the credentials to cut urban pollution, and also offered vastly better fuel economy. Once a more versatile five-door model arrived, Britain's minicab drivers took to it in droves.

▲ *Škoda's renewal continued apace into the 2000s as the excellent VW-based Fabia finally closed the door on the all-Czech Favorit/Felicia series.*

▼ *The Honda Jazz was a fantastic little car that helped blow away Honda's reputation as the geriatric's favourite.*

A car that looked like it should be electric powered – but wasn't – was the Smart City-Coupé, arriving here in 2000. Originating from the people behind the Swatch watch and bankrolled by Mercedes-Benz, the truncated and upright two-seater city runabout featured a tiny 0.8-litre engine at the back, and semi-automatic transmission. Rather than being sold as a cheap and cheerful economy machine, the Smart boasted infinite ways it could be customised and per-sonalised for a higher price, because its easily inter-changeable body panels clipped on to a rigid welded steel cage structure.

The late 1990s car world had been obsessed with 'retro' themes as carmakers attempted to find ways to break free of the identikit herd mentality that logic and economics had dictated. One of the most distinctive was the New Beetle, Volkswagen's bulbous retake on the humble 'People's Car' (*Volks Wagen*). Introduced in 1998, it was now a premium product (using the same platform as the VW Golf and Audi A3) that won approval from gentler motorists, who liked the built-in flower vase in the dashboard, but the scorn of many diehard enthusiasts for its cartoonish appearance. In 2000, Chrysler added to the old-school euphoria with its PT Cruiser, a five-door family hatchback masquerad-ing as a customised 1940s American sedan. It caused a brief, if bemused, stir.

If the X5 wasn't quite the first 'Chelsea tractor' then this luxurious 4x4 BMW certainly got the backs up of anyone on the school run who couldn't afford one ...

In very small cars, Audi thought it had predicted the future with its compact A2 in 1999, a model whose frugality derived from its all-aluminium construction, 1.2-litre engine and carefully finessed aerodynamics. All the science involved, plus high prices, didn't help it to be successful; in contrast, Toyota's 1999 Yaris supermini was an instant hit. Built in a brand-new factory in France, and boasting a wacky hologram instrument display, the Yaris was economical, nimble and proved to be very, very reliable. Advantages like these were also evident in the Škoda Fabia of the same year, the Czech company's Polo-based supermini offering a German car ownership experience at a rock-bottom price. And then shortly after there was yet another small-car hero, the 2001 Honda Jazz, very well regarded both for its interior space and its excellent all-round ability on the road.

It looks dull by recent design standards but the Vauxhall Zafira had something unique to offer – seven seats in a compact MPV package.

One of the last of the classic Minis, a 1.3i, posing opposite the Millennium Dome at London's Greenwich in 2000.

The contemporary 'Chelsea tractor' tag seemed highly appropriate for the 1999 BMW X5, a high-riding and unapologetically expensive off-roader. It was soon a regular on the school run in wealthy towns, enraging as many people as it impressed. No question, though, that it was a highly capable machine – one of the key players in a shift in demand away from conventional luxury cars to ones with commanding driving positions, superb four-wheel drive drivetrains, ample power and the brawn –

while still glittering – to pull a horsebox or speedboat trailer. And yet, the Vauxhall Zafira – its mundane brand name notwithstanding – was even more of a design breakthrough, as designers and engineers managed to squeeze in a row of extra seats to make this the world's first seven-seater compact MPV. They managed to get one over on the idiosyncratic 1998 Fiat Multipla, which had two rows of three seats, but BBC *Top Gear* still made the Italian people-carrier its Car of the Year for 2000.

An exciting new world of Minis lay ahead with BMW, previewed by this first image of the all-new MINI Cooper.

For many, the 2001 X-type was a crossbreed too far, a Jaguar shrunken around a Ford Mondeo base. Viewed dispassionately, though, it was a pretty good car.

Also in 2000, motoring history was made twice by one car. The original Mini, after 5.3m had been sold, came to the end of its road after forty-one years as the very last one was made on 4 October. Then, just a few days later, the all-new MINI (yes, they did spell it all in capitals) was unveiled. BMW had taken the ethos of the original Mini Cooper and reimagined it as a 1.6-litre hatchback for those well-off people not quite ready to start a family.

Controversial it certainly was, and so were the circumstances of its arrival. BMW kept the MINI operation but sold Land Rover off to Ford and Rover cars to its management. This was the trigger for new life to be breathed into the historic MG brand, and in 2001 the renamed MG Rover Group released the ZR, ZS and ZT – performance-orientated MG editions of the Rover 25, 45 and 75 respectively. Coincidentally, in the same year came another new British car that broke the mould. The X-type was a new compact sports saloon from Jaguar, sharing parts with the all-new Ford Mondeo. Most models had four-wheel drive as standard and a high level of equipment, but the shrinking of the classic Jaguar lines to Mondeo proportions created a car guaranteed to polarise opinion – just as much, indeed, as the wild new Morgan Aero 8 which was to take Britain's oldest carmaker still in family ownership into the 2010s and beyond.

All of this shiny new metal might be found by the end of 2003 pounding the smooth new tarmac of the Birmingham North Relief Road, better known as the M6 Toll on which Britain's first road charges for centuries were levied for the privilege of avoiding the daily snarl-up of the Birmingham-skirting M6. But fewer and fewer cars were now going to be found in the gridlocked centre of the capital, where the London Congestion Charge Zone came into operation the same year. At least, that was the plan ...

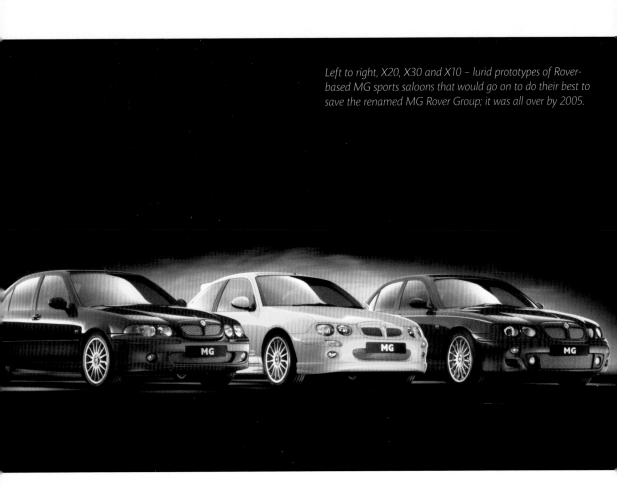

Left to right, X20, X30 and X10 – lurid prototypes of Rover-based MG sports saloons that would go on to do their best to save the renamed MG Rover Group; it was all over by 2005.